022269 2

KU-763-461

B FOD 729

12.50

HOME

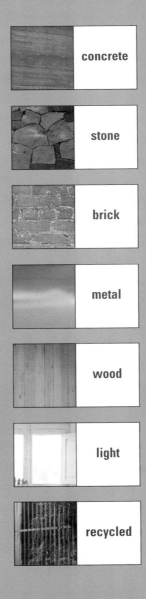

concrete

stone

brick

metal

wood

light

recycled

Publisher: **Paco Asensio**

Editor and Text: **Ana Cristina G. Cañizares**

Documentation: **Lola Gómez**

Art Director: **Mireia Casanovas Soley**

Graphic Design and Layout: **Pilar Cano**

Editorial project:
LOFT Publications
Domènech, 7-9 2° 2ª. 08012 Barcelona. Spain
Tel.: +34 93 218 30 99
Fax: +34 93 237 00 60
loft@loftpublications.com
www.loftpublications.com

2002 © **LOFT** Publications S.L. and HBI,
an imprint of HarperCollins Publishers

First published in 2002 by LOFT and HBI,
an imprint of HarperCollins Publishers
10 East 53rd St. New York, NY 10022-5299

Distributed in the U.S. and Canada by
Watson-Guptill Publications
770 Broadway New York, NY 10003-9595
Telephone: (800) 451-1741 or (732) 363-4511 in NJ, AK, HI
Fax: (732) 363-0338

Distributed throughout the rest of the world by
HarperCollins International
10 East 53rd St. New York, NY 10022-5299
Fax: (212) 207-7654

WG ISBN: 0-8230-2098-3
HBI ISBN: 0-06-051357-8

DL: B-35.339/2002

If you would like to suggest projects for inclusion in
our next volumes, please e-mail details to us at:
loft@loftpublications.com

We have tried our best to contact all copyright
holders. In individual cases where this has not been
possible, we request copyright holders to get in
touch with the publishing house.

All rights reserved. No part of this publication may
be reproduced by any means or procedure, including
photocopying, data-processing and distribution of
samples by renting or by public loan, without the
written authorization of the copyright holders under
the sanctions of the laws currently in force.

HOME

HERTFORD REGIONAL COLLEGE LIBRARY
WARE CENTRE

CONTROL No 185046

4530222692

CLASS No 724 7

SUPPLIER   PRICE
                 12.50 04/04

IN WHATEVER SHAPE OR FORM, THE HOME'S OBJECTIVE HAS ALWAYS BEEN THE SAME: TO SEEK SHELTER FROM THE ELEMENTS IN A PLACE WHICH ONE CAN CALL THEIR OWN

Over thousands of years, human beings have sought refuge in a wide variety of shapes and forms. They have lived in tents, lodges, igloos, pit houses, earth lodges, tepees, treehouses, castles, loghouses and huts. From the earliest cave dwellings to mud houses, medieval castles and to the "modern" homes of today, the objective has always been the same: to seek shelter from the elements in a place which one can call their own.

The evolution of construction has led to the development of endless techniques and materials with which a home can be fabricated. While the earliest shelters were constructed with organic materials like earth, plant fibers, and stone, industrialization and the advent of architecture practice produced an evolution of these kinds of materials into far more structurally complex buildings, using manufactured materials like brick, ceramic, steel and polished stone. Nowadays residential architects continue to use these basic materials, either alone or in combinations. At the same time, we have borne witness to an era of innovation, prompted by ecological factors, in which houses are also being made out of unconventional and recyclable materials.

These advances in architecture translate into contemporary homes with an endless range of possiblities in terms of their exterior and interior design. Sometimes the selection of materials is based on the geographic region and its climate: hotter countries favor tile, concrete or stone, while cold countries opt for wood frame structures with insulating fibers. Light, though not a physical material, is also a vital ingredient for a comfortable and luminous space and often forms the basis for the integral design of a home. Furthermore, the booming "green" movement in architecture is another driving force behind innovative, witty and attractive homes. Still, the selection can be influenced by other factors: how long the structure should last, the cost of production, the restrictions of any location, or simply the aesthetic value held by the architect and client. Undoubtedly in most cases, these and other considerations are taken into account as a whole.

With so many elements to consider and options to choose from, it is no wonder that people may waver when deciding how their home should be built. After all, the home is typically the most valuable possession we own, not only in economic terms but also psychological—as well as being a reference for security and protection, for most people it is a physical manifestion of their creativity, personality and character. In the same way we choose our clothes to express our identity, so does the home express our most cherished values and tastes. GOOD IDEAS: HOME brings together a collection of houses and apartments around the world designed by international contemporary architects, each of them featuring a specific material or concept that stands out in its design. Separate chapters focus on houses in which either concrete, stone, brick, metal, wood, light or recycled materials become the primary feature of each project. Over forty-five examples of residential spaces, in which both exterior construction and interior design display an assortment of styles through the use of precise materials, offer excellent ideas on how to use and combine these elements to create beautiful houses full of originality and character.

Concrete: cement, water, small stones

Advantages: Cost-effective, fireproof, weatherproof, molds to any shape, strong in compression

Disadvantages: Cracks with temperature changes, weak in tension

Although cement has been around for at least 12 million years, the development of concrete as a common building material and its integration into the urban context did not take place until the beginnings of the last century. The first discovered use of the material dates back to 5600 B.C., on the hut flooors of a Yugoslavian stone age village. The Egyptians used it in the construction of the Great Pyramid at Giza in 2500 B.C. It was only in the early 1900´s, however, that its use became normalized and integrated into the modern city. At first, concrete was implemented mostly in larger projects such as high-rise buildings, bridges and structural dams. Cincinnati, Ohio was witness to the first concrete sky-scraper in 1903. Today, concrete is used for any kind of construction, and has become especially popular in the residential sector. It is the favorite of many contemporary architects who have the capability of bringing out the best of such a seemingly plain material, transforming it into a highly aesthetic backdrop for a variety of different styles.

concrete

concrete

GGG HOUSE
Alberto Kalach

Architect: Alberto Kalach, alberto@kalach.com   Photographer: © Undine Pröhl   Location: Mexico DF, Mexico

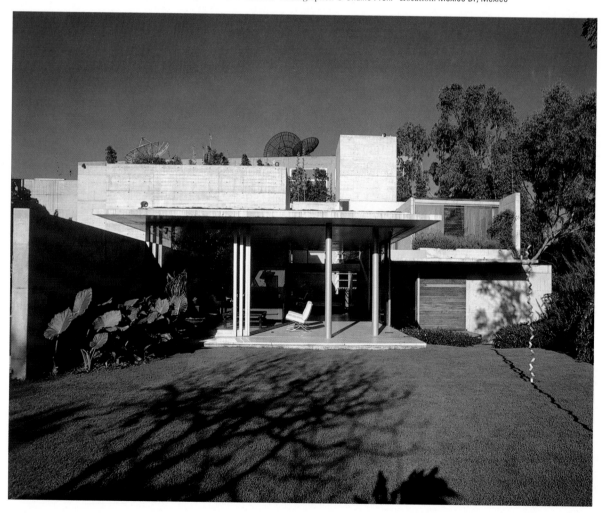

Alberto Kalach is the architect of many well-known residences in Mexico, among them the home of film director Alberto González Iñarritu, through which the GGG project came about. This project realized one of Kalach´s greatest dreams: to construct a residence entirely out of concrete.

The house is a spectacular composition of converging lines and interactive units united by the singular element of concrete. The entrance is accessed from the south side, through a corridor characterized by the horizontality of the concrete paneling and leads to an interior composed of a series of interconnecting rooms, each of which enjoy a space of their own thanks to their clever distribution. They are much like a labyrinth, except that the hallways and corners reveal surprisingly spacious areas drowned in natural light. A sculpture by Jorge Yazpik announces the grandeur of the central hall, where a covered terrace incorporates a lounge area that becomes seamless with the garden by way of large sliding glass panels. The exterior boasts a lush green garden, a carefully designed landscape of bamboo, fig trees, lavender and jacaranda trees. The bedrooms are situated on the first floor, a two-story space intersected by a steel and glass catwalk. A stainless steel kitchen incorporates a continuous counter that looks out at the enveloping trees. The same serenity, elegance and style can be appreciated in the bathroom, on the floor just above.

In every instance, the interior spaces maintain a constant dialogue with the exterior. The children´s bedroom, for example, looks out at eye level onto a breathtaking bed of flowers through a horizontal window that occupies the corner of the room. This relationship with the garden, along with the elegant combination of designer furniture, walnut finishes, and use of warm colors transforms this top-to-botton concrete home into a warm and inviting residence.

A Z chair by Reitveld sits in the bedroom, much more minimalist in design than the rest of the rooms in the house.

The bathroom windows are translucent on the bottom half to maintain privacy from the exterior.

concrete

UP AND DOWN
AV1 Architekten

Architect: AV1 Architekten, info@av1architekten.de Photographer: © Michael Heinrich Location: Kaiserslautern, Germany

This project is situated along a bank of red sandstone quarry remains at the edge of the city center near the Fritz-Walter Stadium. The immediate and significant presence of nature—the red sandstone to the north and a green meadow to the south—dictates the architecture of this housing development containing five autonomous living units.

The theme is architecture versus nature, a concept which stands for all important decisions taken throughout the planning. A rectangular block of three floors incorporates a series of five houses that parallels the wall of red rock. The sedimentation of natural sandstone was the inspiration for the horizontal larch wood panel on the north, east and west sides, imitating the layers that are found in the rock. On the south side, the units open onto a meadow and forest with the help of sliding glass elements between wooden frames. Balconies link the interior to the exterior and also provide protection from the sun during summer months. The roof integrates a gauge system that stores rainwater in a special layer, draining it through the ground without adding to the municipal sewage. Solar panels heat the water.

Inside, the rooms are wrapped in concrete. A hanging staircase slices through the center of the three floors, connecting the separate ceilings in a sweeping, geometric gesture which can be best appreciated from the exterior. This carved-like and lightweight sculptural element and the continuous concrete coverage from floor to ceiling are the unifying elements of each home.

The staircase, which hangs from steel cables, becomes not only a functional structure, but also an aesthetic element that adds a significant dynamic quality to each of the dwellings.

The kitchen, separated
from the dining area by
an island unit, opens onto
a wooden deck terrace.

First floor

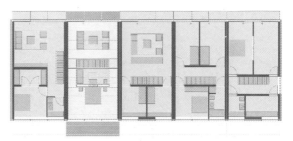

Second floor

CROSS SECTION
Studio Cano Lasso

Architect: Studio Cano Lasso, canolasso@nexo.es   Photographer: © Diego Cano, Ana Carvalho and Pablo Zuloaga   Location: Las Rozas, Madrid, Spain

Located in one of the suburbs on the outskirts of Madrid, this project is the realization of an architect´s goal to build her own home. Having pondered over and developed the idea over various years, Lucia Cano finally built what she was looking for: a conceptual and practical manifestion of her beliefs, desires and needs.

Being a mother of four children, an architect who values her work and her hobbies, and having a special reverance for the relationship between architecture and landscape formed the basis for the evolution of this project. The construction implicates two intersecting horizontal volumes in the shape of a cross. Their horizontality aims to reflect and blend into the succession of horizons that can be seen from the site: a grove of oak trees, followed by the valley, the Galapagar hills, and in the far distance, the mountains that are home to the Escorial Palace. The point at which the two volumes meet create a two-story interior area. The upper volume is a concrete box-like structure that contains a studio and projects itself over a decked terrace, pool and garden. It floats low enough to make the patio feel intimate and to protect the area from heat and sun. The interior spaces are rational, luminous and ample. The flooring is nearly entirely finished in pine, as is the roof terrace of the lower structure.

Despite the weighty appearance of the material, concrete here seems to have taken on a lighter, less solid appearance, mostly thanks to the floor to ceiling windows that occupy its façade. These were recessed deeply from the edges to ensure protection during the summer months so that the studio could continue to enjoy uninterrupted views of the progressive horizon.

Interior view of the intersecting point of the two structures, forming a two-story space that connects the studio with the residence.

The steel rods used in cement structures were kept exposed for their visual aesthetic.

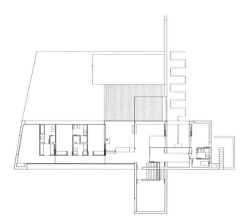

Garden-level plan

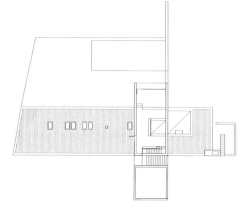

Garage, studio and roof

The office features panoramic views of the continuous landscape and also receives light from a skylight.

concrete

QUAYSIDE LOFT
Jo Crepain

Architect: Jo Crepain, koenraad.janssens@jocrepain.be   Photographer: © Ludo Noël, Jan Verlinde   Location: Antwerp, Belgium

Residential buildings near the harbor are commonly in need of renovation. When two quayside properties became available, architect Jo Crepain was assigned to renovate a recent office building to make room for a city garden and parking garage. The small city garden was linked to three floors of offices and two floors of a loft.

The loft is nearly all finished in concrete, which was used for all new and permanent building fixtures. All the concrete was set in rough casings of veneered three-ply, transferring the pattern of the wood onto the concrete. The symmetric forms created by most of the structure are complemented by curved furniture and accessories in bright primary colors. The ceilings reach thirteen feet in height and amplify the sense of space. A staircase occupies the central core, painted entirely in black to contrast with the adjacent white walls and white furniture pieces like the sofa and bed. This resulted in a coarse finish punctuated at regular intervals with casing holes, an effect which contrasts nicely with the smooth appearance of the aluminum furnishings.

Distributed in a way so that doors become unnecessary, areas like the kitchen, bedroom and library occupy a space of their own without losing any fluidity between them. In the kitchen, a long stainless steel island receives natural light that pours in through large, square windows from overhead. The bedroom area is separated by a white partition to provide privacy, and the library is open to the living area, occupying the entire far wall. The living room, its façade clad with floor to ceiling glass windows, opens onto a decked terrace with splendid views of the city harbor. The project is a very modern and fluid home whose use of concrete in combination with other textures and tones creates a warm, comforting and inviting space.

View of the central staircase area: Unlike the concrete ceilings in the living area, the ceilings here and in the bedroom are vaulted restored brick varnished in white.

First level

Second level

concrete

NINE UNITS
Yamaoka Design Studio

Architect: Yamaoka Design Studio, y-ikeda@yamaoka-architects.co.jp   Photographer: © Nacása & Partners   Location: Tokyo, Japan

This project is a small, nine-unit collective housing building in the metropolitan area of Tokyo. This type of housing permits the tenants to choose their residence according to social changes, family matters, lifestyle, values, personal economic conditions, etc., offering many advantages to the client. This housing complex aims to provide a temporary living space for people who enjoy an urban lifestyle.

The building´s concrete, glass and steel frame façade presents three vertical units that project from the main structure. The interior is almost entirely faced in concrete. All units feature a thick stainless steel island dining counter that measures twelve feet in length that serves a variety of uses, from everyday use to buffet-style parties. The bathroom is situated in the center, flanked by a mini-atrium on both sides, in which an airshaft was created to maximize natural light and ventilation. Bamboo was planted inside these atriums to create the sensation of nature. The exterior and interior finishes are both concrete, with a smooth water-resistant finish. The interior floors consist of insulation, a hot-water floor heating system and a mesh-blended mortar and steeping-type water-resistant finish.

The narrow quarters have been optimally distributed to take the best advantage of the available space. The successive order of the functions, such as the bathroom and kitchen, create an interesting perspective from one side or the other. Separated by sliding translucent glass doors, the areas can be opened up to reveal this continuous succession or closed off to retain the privacy of each individual area. Concrete is accompanied mainly by glass, steel and the presence of greenery, which softens the ambience and lends a comforting and contemporary environment.

View from the bottom of the building up through the openings in between the housing units.

concrete

BETWEEN HEAVEN AND EARTH
Alberto Campo Baeza

Architect: Alberto Campo Baeza, campo-baeza@redestb.es   Photographer: © Hisao Suzuki   Location: Madrid, Spain

A spectacular piece of architecture, this project by Alberto Campo Baeza yields the limelight to the true object of its purpose: the unsurpassable beauty of the surrounding landscape. Sober, austere and unpretentious, this building anchors itself to the ground and simultaneously reaches up towards the heavens. A solid concrete shell is the base for an ethereal glass structure that defies the boundaries between interior and exterior.

The rectangular concrete base sits on top of a sloping terrain surrounded by a flourishing green landscape. The main façade, punctured by large, square windows, contains the bedrooms, living room and dining room. The service area, bathrooms and traffic areas are situated at the rear, where light filters through smaller openings in the upppermost part of the wall. The glass structure atop the concrete ceiling is a vantage point accessible from inside the house. The supporting frame consists of eight double columns with a U-shaped section. Its roof, a sheet of white-painted steel, is the only part of the frame that comes into contact with the glass panelling, which appears to be seamless. The roof extends farther than the glass refuge on either side so that there is a shaded porch that offers protection from the strong sunlight. At one end, a swimming pool is embedded into the concrete, and during daylight induces countless reflections that play over the exterior walls and roof.

The use of concrete for such a large and austere structure creates a straightforward expression that is neither ostentatious nor conspicuous. Its pure and linear form blends with the surounding terrain in an attempt to connect architecture and nature. The contrast between density and lightness, solidity and transparency becomes evident in the joining of concrete and glass. In this project, it is a marriage of elements that adheres to the ground, floats towards the sky and embraces the beauty that envelops it.

Above: View of the main façade that faces north towards the mountains. The glass structure is practically imperceptible to the eye.

Right: View of the rear façade. Here one can see the concrete base partially inserted into the sloping hill, as if a refuge emerging from the landscape.

Below right: Unlike the glass belvedere, the lower level is a solid unit. The northern façade has large square openings which create panoramic views from the living areas inside.

Northern elevation

Western elevation

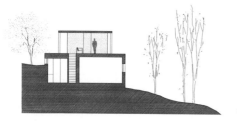

Cross-section

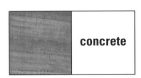

concrete

BALANCING ACT
Ángel Sánchez Cantalejo + Vicente Tomás

Architect: Ángel Sánchez Cantalejo + Vicente Tomás   Photographer: © Alejo Bagué   Location: Santa Margarita, Mallorca, Spain

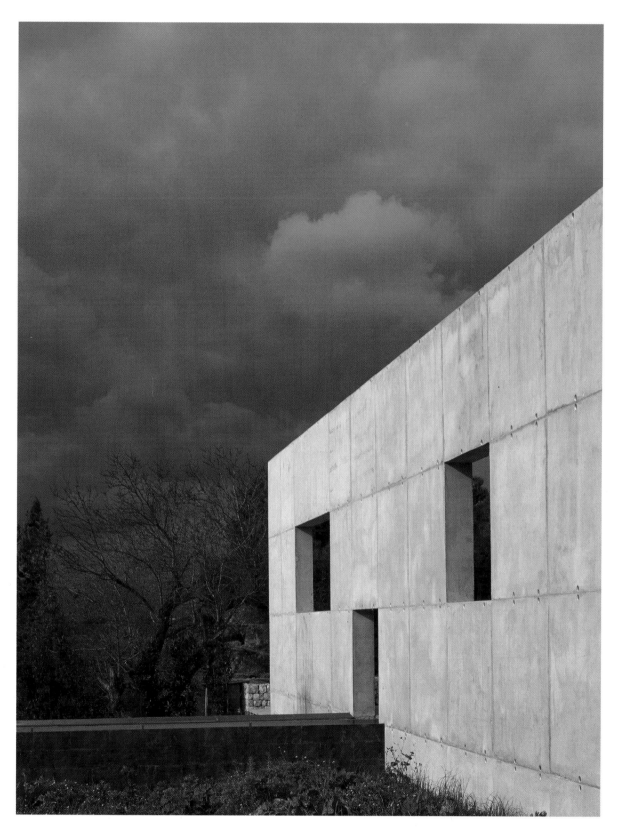

This stunning house is situated on the flat and outstretched terrain of Santa Margarita on the island of Mallorca, Spain. Close to the sea yet surrounded by grassland, the house enjoys magnificent views of land and sea. The composition is defined, straightforward and linear; its rooms are distinct and marked by their shape and material. It is evident that the architect has studied its visual composition just as a painter composes the subjects of a painting.

The structure is defined by a concrete base that wraps around the interior and exterior. A wooden deck marks the entrance through a passage covered by a concrete roof. A small garden lies before the front door, and can be seen from the inside through large glass windows. The living and dining areas are located on this ground floor which looks out towards the façade windows and over the long, rectangular pool and decked terrace. The concrete wall wraps around one corner of the plot, containing a large, landscaped patio, laid in concrete slabs and punctuated by trees and grassed areas. Some edges are bordered by a pocket of small pebbles, to soften the feel of the concrete. The second volume constitutes the second floor, which sits on top of the base, slightly to one side. A window on the other side balances the composition. This entity is furnished in narrow wooden planks, their horizontality emphasizing the direction of the landscape. It contains the private areas of the residence, including the bedrooms and bathrooms.

Straight lines, squares and rectangles are used to balance the volumes. Windows, doors, and walls act as weights, positioned so that the composition remains balanced. Openings in the concrete walls guide the eye through a framed view of the landscape beyond. Just as the project embraces the landscape as a work of art, so does it intend to find that sort of balance in architecture.

The upper volume incorporates a terrace for the bedrooms.

The guest bedroom speaks the same language as the structure: simplicity, balance and beauty.

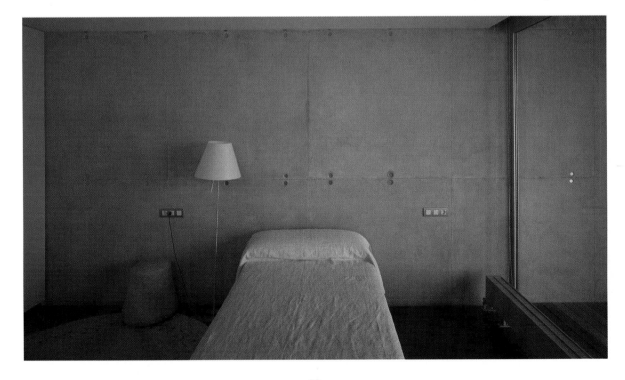

Stone: varied minerals

Advantages: strong in compression, fireproof, weatherproof, resistant, durable, insulator

Disadvantages: heavy, weak in tension

From the dawn of civilization stone has been an essential part of the building blocks of history. The pyramids of Egypt, the Taj Mahal, Stonehenge, the Coliseum in Rome, all encapsulate the history of this natural material. Available in a wide variety of colors, textures and densities, the most common types used in homes include marble, granite, sandstone and slate. Stone is another of those ancient materials that continues to be popular in residential architecture today. Fortunately, and unlike our ancestors, we are spared from having to carry loads of it without machinery. Its hardness, durability and variability offers many advantages. It is also a safe and practical material that ensures warmth in the cold and freshness in heat. Depending on the way it is treated, stone can be used to lend a more rustic home or indeed a very modern and minimalist structure. It can be cut, polished or left as-found, offering innumerable possibilites to the architect and client.

stone

BARE ESSENTIALS
Bedmar & Shi

Architect: Bedmar & Shi, bedmar.shi@pacific.net.sg   Photographer: © Bedmar & Shi Location: Queen Astrid Park, Singapore

The design of this stone-clad house is based on the architects' ongoing mission to provide contemporary expressions of traditional Asian architecture, while still addressing the simple purity of a modern style. The result is a highly-disciplined language of lightness and simplicity that supports the expression of the construction as a tropical, porous envelope. The neutrality of the design is also detectable in the skillful handling of shape and form.

The house constitutes an arrangement of masses around a central courtyard space. The structure can be read as a series of layers that also act as filters. The first layer is the driveway which is flanked by numerous walls and landscaped areas. The second layer is made up of the bridge, water pond and garden. The third layer is a two-story corridor that leads to the elegant living room, the family sleeping quarters and the main two-story pavilion. Throughout, there is a sense of equilibrium expressed through juxtapositions between foreground, midground and background, their introductions expressing a quiet and dynamic balance.

A restrained palette of materials and colors was used to express lightness and simplicity. Stone is the primary dominating element, along with white walls and light wood floors. The house embraces intimacy with its tropical surroundings and also protects the interior from the harsh climatic conditions. Heat and ventilation were handled through careful orientation in relation to the sun as well as through the use of slender rectangular masses. The designer's ultimate wish is to reduce architecture to the essential components for shade and shelter. In this case, although the components were not reduced, the architects demonstrate possibilities that aspire towards the reduction of architecture to its most essential, pure and distilled form.

The geometric patterns created by the cuts in the stone are reflected in the shape of the furniture, in this case the dining table and chairs.

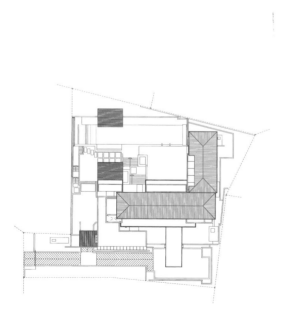

Roof plan

The steps that lead down to
the basement level are broken
by a patch of green grass.

stone

WING SPAN
Enrique Browne

Architect: Enrique Browne, ebrowne@entelchile.net Photographer: © Guy Wenborne + Enrique Browne Location: Zapallar, Chile

The plot of land on which this house was built presented various complications due to its inclination from north to south and certain construction regulations particular to the area. Various solutions revolving around its orientation, distribution and the materials used contributed to the success of the project, blessed with magnificent views of the ocean and bay.

Due to the slope of the land, the site received little sunlight. It was imperative, however, that the building should not exceed twenty-four and a half feet parallel to the ground, which led the architect to situate the house as far north as possible. Having done this, there needed to be a way of composing the home so that the right area received as much light as possible. So as to not infringe on the mentioned height regulation, the architect devised a program of interconnecting volumes on three separate levels that span out like the feathers of a bird's wing, or the leaves of a branch. The house can be perceived as flying over its own terrain, at the same time mimicking the green landscape through its green copper-coated walls. The stone used to level the building, and for its interiors is typical of the region.

The three volumes are linked by ramps flanked in glass, its zigzagging route offering varying perspectives of the house and the town. On the north side, the house is clad in translucent thermal panels, which at night transform into a sort of horizontal light source. The master bedroom is situated on the highest level, the children's bedroom on the lowest level, and the kitchen and living area in between. The regional stones and aged green copper used in the construction integrate the contemporary lines of the design into the surrounding landscape.

The living room occupies the intermediate "wing" of the three volumes and points towards the bay, of which it has a privileged view.

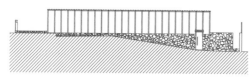

North elevation

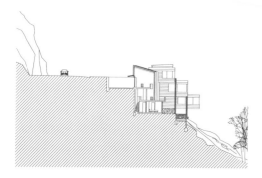

Cross-section

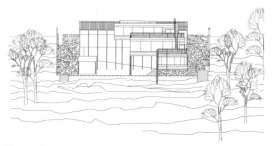

South elevation

stone

SICILIAN TAVERN

Photographer: © Adriano Brusaforri Location: Pantelleria, Italy

This home on the Italian island of Pantelleria off the coast of Sicily emerges from the stone and lush green landscape that surrounds it. Its simple lines and solid stone construction are typical to the architecture of the region. The rocks disappear into the trees, plants and flowers that crop up along the borders of the house, camouflaging the structure that peers out over the mountains towards the sea.

Irregular blocks of light and dark stones are combined to form the sturdy walls that enclose the living space. Cane and reed are used to make some of the roofs and other functional pieces. On the porch, pillows and cushions are placed on a cement block and used as a sofa, and straw mats are placed underneath to soften the hardenss of the cement. Inside, simplicity defines the decorative statement. The bedroom walls have been finished in a smooth cement coating where the underlying stone becomes visible in an aperture that acts as a night table. The walls were given a crackled, aged effect and tinted with subtle blotches of color that match with the Oriental-like color scheme of the interior. The bathroom features an extraordinary shower carved out of the stone structure, irregular in shape and decorated with tiny mosaic pieces in random places.

The implementation of stone, in this case untreated, reminds one of antiquity, protection and coolness. The raw state of the stone is a tribute to ancient architecture, and its density assures us of its durability and capacity of keeping a house cool in the hottest months of the year. It is also a material that in its most natural state can aesthetically contribute to both the interior and exterior of a space.

Top: Using a traditional local technique, the inside of this laundry sink was covered with decorative ceramic tiles.

Above: Most of the rooms in the house use fabric in place of doors. This blue cotton curtain acts as a window outside one of the bedrooms, providing shade from the strong sunlight.

Right: View through an arched ceiling of the square stone fireplace in the living area. The absence of excess elements enhances the forms and materials employed.

The kitchen is modest and functional: only the basics are necessary for a natural lifestyle.

Natural objects and Mediterranean influences are part of the decoration of this seaside villa, visible in and around every corner.

stone

LAID IN STONE
Thomas Wegner

Architect: Thomas Wegner, thomaswegner@gmx.de   Photographer: © Pere Planells Location: Mallorca, Spain

A long path of twigs, fallen leaves and dense greenery leads to a large country house on the island of Mallorca, Spain. This large block was erected in stone, which can be best appreciated in its principle façade; a linear, austere block of rock punctured by two small windows and a main arched doorway. The structure is encircled by a stone wall with a small wooden gate that gives access into the property.

Architect Thomas Wegner brought his ideas and sketches to life with the help of island craftsmen in giving shape to iron, wood and stone for the interior of this atmospheric home. The careful mixture of rural and modern show through in the lighting and minimal detail of the decoration. Contemporary glass windows, as well as the lamps and lighting systems used are evidence of the implementation of practical modern-day appliances to lend functionality and comfort, as well as an aesthetic contrast to the age-old structure. Rustic details can be found in the kitchen, where a stained pine beam and indigenous reed ceiling hovers high over a sturdy iroko wood table with matching benches. The floor consists of rounded stones set in cement and the countertop is green terrazo. Two adjustable light rails that finish in spotlights offer an interesting contrast in form and style. In the bedrooms and living area, simplicity and minimalism come to the fore. White walls, translucent fabrics and few accessories create a cool and soothing environment.

Many of the walls inside the house were made out of polished cement colored with island soil. Nevertheless the presence of stone reveals itself throughout the interior and most impressively in its exterior. The substantial construction and its timeworn presence give it a warmth and personality which is only enhanced by its spectacular natural surroundings.

Top: A minimalist-style stone staircase that climbs up alongside one of the walls connects the two levels.

Above: These new iron-framed glass doors are a practical and attractive solution for weathered old structures. They provide better insulation and add a fresh look to the space.

Left: The rocks found around the house have been eroded over time by torrents of water. Climbing the naturally-formed steps, one can appreciate an excellent view of the house´s typical Mallorcan exterior.

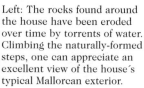

stone

IBIZA ON DISPLAY
Víctor Espósito

Architect: Víctor Espósito   Stylist: Ino Coll   Photographer: © Pere Planells   Location: Ibiza, Spain

Victor Espósito, the architect of this project in Ibiza, brought together old and new themes to create a rural minimalism within an old stone structure typical to the architecture of the island. The presence of nature in the form of natural materials, plants and earth tones characterizes the interior and exterior of this home. Much of the stone structure was preserved and kept exposed to exhibit its aesthetic potential.

White predominates on the inside walls the house and serves as a canvas for furniture pieces that include chairs, sculptures, paintings, and vases. Various doorways, for example in the bedroom, take on a Moorish character while others are perfectly contemporary in form and material, such as those in the living room that open out onto the main terrace. Besides stone, there is a great presence of wood, iron and woven fabrics.

The stone becomes evident throughout various places in the house. In the bedroom, it is emphasized to by two narrow encrusted pebble stripes along the floor that unite the raised area where the bed is located with the rest of the bedroom area. Near the entrance, the exposed stone walls envelop a great tree trunk that sprouts from the floor and up through the roof. The kitchen´s weather-beaten character takes on a purely aesthetic role and contrasts with the smooth white walls. In the bathroom a stone sink emerges out of the surface as if overflowing. The stone structure can be best appreciated from the outside, which is made up of a central rectangular swimming pool and various terraces bordered by stone walls. Thatched roofs covered with palm leaves and supported by wooden beams are the setting for an intimate lounge area made comfortable with pillows and mattresses. There is no lack of cozy corners from where to look out over the stunning horizon.

Left: A unique lounge chair made from thick tree branches held together by an intricately woven yarn.

Right: A Moorish door leads to the master bedroom´s ensuite bathroom.

stone

QUINTA SANTO OVÍDIO
Álvaro Siza

Architect: Álvaro Siza, siza@mail.telepac.pt Photographer: © Duccio Malagamba Location: Oporto, Portugal

About a forty minute drive from Siza's hometown of Oporto lies this country weekend home in the midst of the Duoro region and its winding lanes, vineyards, streams and stone walls. Rarely having very much time for small-scale projects like this one, the architect was drawn to it for the fact that the house belonged to an old friend and by the prospect of being able to work closely with good local craftsmen.

The Quinta retains the core of the original farmhouse. The entrance features a baroque gate and a fountain with an enormous and elaborately carved granite back-piece. A roughly paved entry court leads to the L-shaped house surrounded by a lush garden, camellia trees, a few towering palm trees and a restored stone fountain. The granite walls of the main house, which once contained animal stalls on the ground floor and living quarters above, had to be largely reconstructed to its original state. The architect placed the bedrooms on the ground floor and the living room, kitchen/dining room and library on the upper floor. One of the new additions includes the chapel created for the wedding of Siza's daughter. The twelve by eighteen feet space, with its minimalist design dotted by rustic and antique pieces, effortlessly transcends solemnity, reflection and illumination, its presence matching the grandeur of an ancient baroque church.

The project demonstrates the architect's intuitive ability to integrate the modern architecture for which he is known into a purely rural and baroque construction that dates back to the eighteen century. The treatment of stone, whether restored or new, remains true to the origins of the house. Siza fuses his formal style with the surviving local craft traditions, resulting in a highly modern residence in concept, yet completely authentic in practice, reflecting the culture and traditions of its native land.

Opposite: The magical chapel features semicircular and cross-shaped windows and a pair of sycamore chairs designed by Siza.

stone

PADLEY MILL
Peter Blundell Jones

Architect: Peter Blundell Jones, p.blundelljones@sheffield.ac.uk   Photographer: © Peter Blundell Jones   Location: Derbyshire, UK

Previously a mill at the bottom of Padley Gorge that was added onto over the centuries, the decrepit building was bought by the architects in 1994 with the aim of transforming it into a country house. The objective was to retain two essential elements: the gritstone walls and slate roof that date back to medieval times.

The interior virtually disintegrated, the architects put in a new steel joist to support the sagging timber beams on the first floor. Metal windows were replaced with oak-framed ones, and most notably a two-story cut was made in the north wall. Because the site slopes steeply from north to south, the building appears to be three stories high at the front and two at the back. The big cut in the garden wall introduces light into the center of the volume, illuminating what was once a very dark space. Upstairs, a thick window beyond the kitchen looks out into a long narrow pool lined with massive stone slabs. The adjustable water level can sometimes reach nearly the top of the window, making the room seem like an under-water cave. The interior is lined with recycled paper insulation, and the new woodwork is in solid beech. The front door is made of three wide planks of oak, bound together with galvanized strap hinges.

All new stone was found on-site and was dressed and laid by local craftsmen. The project solidly adheres to its original structure and purpose, integrating contemporary detailing that self-consciously reworks the structure in a late twentieth century manner. The architects say that they have "aestheticized" the mill, made the pond an object of contemplation and turned the industrial vernacular into a new kind of brutalist minimalism. This dialogue produced a rich and engaged design that was made possible by the relationship maintained with its historical past.

The stone of the area is called gritstone, or millstone grit, which constitutes the whole hill where the mill is located. It is a kind of sandstone with very hard grains, fairly robust and varying in color from grey-brown to almost pink.

Brick: burned clay

Advantages: cost-effective, long-lasting, strong in compression

Disadvantages: heavy, weak in tension

Brick is one of the planet's oldest building materials. Only the basic elements are needed to produce it: earth, water and fire. For this reason it is probably the most environmental material, being both resourceful and recyclable. Bricks are made by shaping a plastic mass of clay and water which is then hardened by drying and firing. In the mid-1800's, steam power turned this purely manual process into a mechanized system that evolved into mass-production. As the simplest and most ancient construction material, it continues to be used in architecture as one of the most trustworthy, elegant and stylish on the market. Aside from its load-bearing properties and aesthetic appeal, brick is economic for not requiring any surface treatment and for its immeasurable durability. Architects often discover brick concealed underneath the walls of abandoned spaces and industrial sites which they uncover and leave exposed for their character and visual appeal. In cities like New York, Barcelona and Berlin it is not uncommon to find brick inside some of the fashionable homes designed by the most contemporary architects.

brick

brick

CENTER OF ATTENTION
Grollmitz-Zappe

Architect: Grollmitz-Zappe, info@grollmitz-zappe-architekten.de   Photographer: © Kirsti Kriegel   Location: Prenzlauer Berg, Berlin, Germany

This Berlin flat takes full advantage of its original and primary constructive element. Situated on the third floor of a late nineteenth century industrial brick building, the interior brickwork has been left completely exposed, as was the building´s façade. Full of light and spatial flexibility, the space is an uncommon composition of unique and interesting forms.

Wrapped in red brick walls, a vaulted brick ceiling, and a polished cement floor, the apartment stands out for its minimal yet striking design. Brick becomes the backdrop for a series of modular furniture that can be moved around to suit different purposes. In the center of the space lies the star of the project: an unconventional bathroom pod held within a sculpted metallic wire mesh, whose translucency depends on the light it receives. Inside is the toilet, shower, and a small washbasin, while another faucet and basin module remain just outside of the structure. The container, not only functional, becomes decorative, especially with the dramatic lighting system incorporated for nightime.

While the bathroom and living area occupy one half of the space, the other half is ocupied by the kitchen and dining area. Three separate and mobile kitchen units make it possible to transform a cooking space into an informal eating area. The large amount of surface area and the presence of mobile furniture creates the possibility for rearranging the distribution. To assure the authenticity of the materials and emphasize their aesthetic potential, any electrical wiring, sockets, switches and heating were set in the cement floor. The winding light rails reinstate the interaction between curved and straight lines and in several graceful gestures unify the space from one side to the other.

A free-standing basin unit incorporates a storage space without occupying much room inside the bathroom pod.

One of the walls is decorated with a mural, adding color and personality to the brick walls.

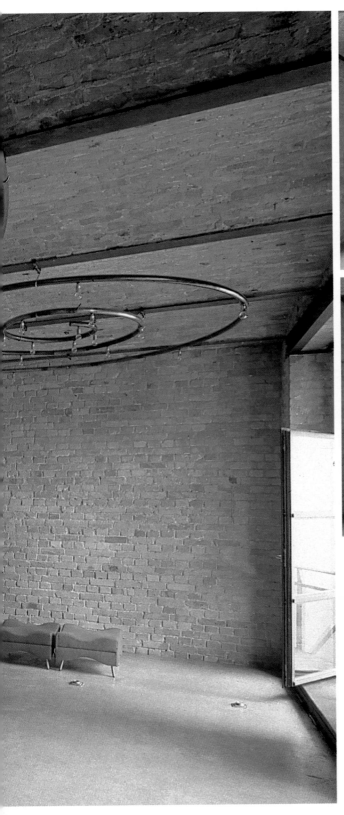

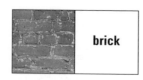

brick

MEETING POINT
Mike Haas

Architect: Mike Haas   Photographer: © Wini Sulzbach   Location: Berlin, Germany

In an attempt to preserve the character of the original building in which this apartment in Berlin is located, most of the brick walls were kept intact and left exposed. Brick is combined with white walls and light wood floors, creating a continuous communication between these elements, mingling and meeting one another through various forms inside the apartment.

The conservatory, nearly eighteen feet in height, opens onto a large terrace accessed by a spiral staircase next to the open kitchen area. Skylights were placed in the living areas, bedroom and bathroom, taking advantage of the apartment´s ideal setting and flooding it with natural light. The original brick structure led the architect to insert a cozy reading corner onto a raised platform that is reached by wooden steps.

In the attic-like space, several of the façade walls are inclined, a feature which was translated into some of the elements inside the home. The fireplace, for example, which had to be moved to comply with building regulations, was placed adjacent to one of the brick columns. Its four sides converge to a point as they rise up the side of the column, echoing the angled ceilings. Similarly, the brick surfaces merge into the white walls, revealing themselves underneath a layer of white paint which appears to have been scraped off at random to expose the underlying structure. This imperfect look is an attractive way to blend different materials, accentuating the presence of a particular material by way of a simple and original technique.

The kitchen area is marked by a tiled surface that visually distinguishes it from the surrounding living room.

Brick is a match for any style. Here, comfortable leather sofas and chairs are combined with ethnic rugs and simple furniture.

The pitched ceiling was opened up and fitted with windows to bring in as much light as possible. The glass doors lead onto a small balcony.

The fireplace takes on an interesting shape that once again merges new elements within the original structure.

brick

SHAKEN NOT STIRRED
Döring Dahmen Joeressen Architekten

Architect: Döring Dahmen Joeressen Architekten, info@ddj.de Collaborators: Bernhard Korte Photographer: © Manos Meisen Location: Italy

This rural home sits on top of a small hill amidst the Italian countryside. Its geographic location renders it vulnerable to earthquakes, which meant that its design had to take this risk into consideration. The best solution was to build a reinforced concrete frame covered by brick walls that would ensure rigidity and stability.

The supporting system is arranged on a fifteen-foot grid that dictates the layout of the house. The entire outer structure is finished in brick and coated in native tufa, a volcanic material noted for its porous quality and heavy structure. The thickness granted by the layering of materials increases the building's ability to keep it cool in summer and retain heat during the winter months. The house is composed of two levels along a sloping terrain, and the lower contains an office and rooms designated for farming activities. The upper level, partly at ground level due to the inclination of the land, contains the domestic spaces and a large terrace.

One of the main goals of the project was to minimize construction details so that the structure could speak for itself. Expert local artisans became involved to help solve certain technical problems. The linear forms and right angles of the structure's exterior are what characterize the house. These are contrasted by the rounded, organic shapes that surround it, most notably in the garden, which Bernhard Korte designed with the careful selection of plants and trees. The brick structure, punctured by a symmetrical series of windows, has a light color and porous texture that counteract the solidity and heaviness of the material. The final product is a clear demonstration of a solution that has been carefully executed to attain both technical and aesthetic results.

Top: An exterior patio is protected from the sunlight by trees and a slatted roof.

Above: The windows and doors are recessed into the structure, allowing space for shutters to shield the sun and heat.

Opposite: Looking closely, one can see the intricate texture of the volcanic/brick material. Irregular pores and brushstrokes add a dynamic textural quality to the all-encompassing element.

The interior spaces are as unadorned as the exterior. Right angles and geometric shapes dominate white and luminous rooms.

brick

LITTLE ALHAMBRA
Charles Boccara

Architect: Charles Boccara, archiboc@iam.net.ma Photographer: © Pere Planells Location: Marrakech, Morocco

Charles Bocarra´s love for Moroccan style translates into this authentic vacation home constructed using local methods. The house is located in the Palm Gardens, on the outskirts of Marrakech, encircled by a carpet of green grass and waving palm trees. The project reinvents a traditional Moroccan palace full of structural details that echo the architecture, style and ambience of times past.

The project is focused around the use of ceramic, in the form of tile along the floors and a brick effect along some of the walls and pillars. This brick effect can be seen on the columns that frame the entrance of the building, across domed ceilings and around arched doors. The material used is not conventional brick, but a technique using ceramic pieces—much like the ones found along the floors—that affords an appearance very similar to that of laid brick. They are encrusted with cement to form the desired pattern and are best displayed inside the bath and main living room. In the stone bath, an entire wall displays this craft, and on the ceiling the pattern is broken by a series of small, round skylights that filter narrow rays of sunlight into the space. Similarly, the dome in the living room culminates in an intricately designed glass top.

Employing traditional construction methods like these produced the authenticity of this sheltered hideaway. Much of the contemporary furniture, pictures and accessories were imported from France, while other pieces were designed by Bocarra himself and manufactured in Morocco. Handicrafts and restored antiques are also part of the interior design, where elegance and traditional detail turn a reinvented space into an authentic Moorish oasis.

Top: The bedrooms exude simplicity and pay attention to Moorish detail.

Above: Contrasting styles mingle effortlessly, such as a European sculpture of a ballerina placed on a shelf and a Moroccan stone fountain decorated by a border of geometric tiles.

Left: Some of the exterior doors are highly valuable, being antique originals that were restored by the owner to contribute to the authenticity of the overall design.

brick

SHOWER ON STAGE
Blockarchitecture

Architect: Blockarchitecture, graeme@blockarchitecture.com   Photographer: © Chris Tubbs Location: London, UK

The design of this loft in London demonstrates the architects' interest in redirecting the experience, the space, and its materials toward new configurations within the contemporary "snip and cut" cultural context. The idea was to allow the concrete and brick frame, which defines and contains the entire space, to be as complete and open as possible.

The dimensions and form of the shell are emphasized by the strong relief of the wood floor, cut to fit the main flow of space toward the balconies on the east front of the building. A thirty-foot wall built of recycled steel panels dominates and organizes the residence, defining a hall, a small storeroom, a bathroom separate from the toilet and a photographer's darkroom. Spotlights fitted underneath this structure lend an indirect ambient light that signals the entrance into the contained area. The remaining household functions, including the kitchen and bath, are located beside the opposite wall. The shower and bathroom occupy a special place raised on a platform of concrete that floats above the wood floor. The area has no partition walls or curtains, demonstrating an unconventional approach to the privacy of bathroom space. The distribution of storage along two sides enables the apartment to become a large open area which can be used for many different activities without having to establish either sleeping quarters or a formal living room.

While some walls and structural columns were restored, many were left exposed and intact. Their rough, sparsely plastered brick surfaces create an informal and stylish environment. The walls themselves are decorative objects that contribute an industrial character to the loft space. The mixture of recycled pieces, contemporary furnishings and antique fittings like the bathtub tie together well against the exposed brick walls and smooth wood floors.

The kitchen is a modern, stainless steel unit which is both practical and attractive.

The recycled steel panels, much like the brick walls, offer an aesthetic value along with the purpose that they serve as partitions.

brick

SLIDING DOORS
Cho Slade

Architect: Cho Slade, choslade@mindspring.com Photographer: © Jordi Miralles Location: New York, New York, USA

The conversion of industrial spaces into lofts is a common architectural venture in the city of New York. This results in the incorporation of existing materials, such as brick, into residential projects, offering an alternative to bare white walls or restored surfaces. This residence maximizes the presence of its old brick structure, making it the main attraction of the loft space.

Massive eight-inch thick exposed brick walls extend the full length of the apartment. The central core contains the kitchen, study and master bathroom, around which the dining area, living room and master bedroom sit. As a contrast to the heavy stationary brick walls, translucent materials such as acid-etched glass were used to construct the ceiling, walls and doors, revealing the shadows of internal pipes and mechanical equipment. The space features a clever distribution, organized using multi-purpose furniture. A large sliding pantry opens to enclose the study, a sliding panel discreetly disguised as a background for black and white photographs conceals a cloakroom, and in the bedroom a walk-in closet doubles as a headboard with built-in reading lights and night tables.

The rough texture and worn appearance of the exposed brick is softened by the smooth textures and sleek forms of the leather furniture, polished wooden surfaces and stainless steel kitchen. A chalkboard in the kitchen area poses a fun and practical solution in keeping with the informal yet always stylish character of the loft. Two arched doorways that lead to the bedrooms display the thickness of the massive brick walls.

View of the sliding pantry in the kitchen area. When open, it serves as a partition to the office study. It can be closed to permit the entry of light from the façade windows.

Soft textures supplied by the furniture and floors balance the roughness of the brick walls.

Translucent glass and sliding doors also furnish the apartment. The bathroom is practical and functional.

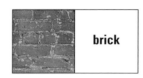

brick

EX POST
by the residents

Interior design: by the residents   Photographer: © Ole Kruger   Location: Berlin, Germany

This loft is located in an old neighborhood of East Berlin called Prenzlauer Berg. The space is situated in a former post office building that was vacant for five years prior to its conversion into various rooms. The four current tenants discovered the building in 1998 and decided to rent the first floor, which was once the post office's administrative department.

The 3,230 square-foot floor was separated into five areas—each of the tenants created a private 270 square-foot room, while the remaining space was left for communal use, including the living, cooking and eating areas. The building's structural brick columns were preserved and left as they were found. They can be appreciated from both the façade and the interior, their worn and aged appearance giving a special character to the space within its historical context. The original metal front doors were also retained for their aesthetic value and reference to the space's original function.

Inside, the decoration is a mélange of different decades, with an emphasis on fifties culture. The kitchen features a unique metal structure that acts as a bar and breakfast table. Concrete slabs make up most of the flooring, and large windows fill the space with natural light. The old cabling and heating pipes that run along the ceiling, still used today, were left exposed for their visual attractiveness. This, along with the simple furniture, exposed brick columns, patchy paintwork and mixture of curious objects make for an informal and stylish urban residence.

An original vintage bar sign purchased from a local flea market decorates the kitchen bar, which is situated behind a curved metal structure with matching stools.

Modern art, dresses on mannequins and an original foosball table form part of the decoration in this imaginative space.

Metal: iron, other variants depending on the type

Advantages: very strong in tension and compression

Disadvantages: rusts, loses strength in extremely high temperatures

Industrialization introduced the use of metal in architecture in the second half of the 19th century. Different types of metal with varying compositions are designated for different purposes. Steel, for example, comprised of iron with a touch of carbon, is one of the strongest materials in construction, most often used for the suspension cables in bridges, trusses and beams, columns in skyscrapers and on rollercoaster tracks. Cast iron is comprised of iron with lots of carbon, molds to any shape, but is weaker than steel in tension, which means that it can break without warning. Aluminum is an alloy that contains magnesium and copper. It is far lighter than steel and iron, does not rust and is also strong in compression and tension. Although during the industrial revolution this was a relatively cheap material, at present it is somewhat costly. Iron and steel´s corrosive tendency keep maintenance costs high and the need for metal surfaces to be constantly painted and coated with a protective layer. Despite its disadvantages, metal continues to be a widely used material, both for its physical strength and it highly modern and aesthetic potential.

me
tal

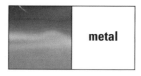

metal

LUXURY CELL
Johnson Chou

Architect: Johnson Chou, mail@johnsonchou.com   Photographer: © Wolker Seding Photography   Location: Toronto, Canada

When Eric Yolles, son of renowned Canadian structural engineer Morden Yolles, asked designer Johnson Chou to renovate 1000 square feet of his loft space located in Toronto´s Merchandise Lofts, he asked him to "think penitentiary." With a great deal of intuition, skill and grace, Johnson Chou managed to instill the characteristics of discipline, order and clarity which the client desired in his home.

In dividing the large open space, Chou drew on the common notions of a prison cell: raw material, surveillance and the absence of excess. For this reason, Chou began by removing all non-structural walls and introducing a large thirty-foot sandblasted screen to divide the main space. In addition, he layered the space with sliding partitions, the largest one being a dramatic sixteen-foot section of stainless steel that separates the bedroom from the living area. In the bedroom, an aluminum-clad king-sized bed cantilevered from the wall floats before a wall of floor-to-ceiling aluminum closets that span the length of the room. Through a ten-inch strip of clear glass along the bathroom doors, Chou indulges in a voyeuristic view of the sunken slate bathtub from the living area. The platform on which the wet areas are located are clad in blue-green slate and distinguished by a sculptural, freestanding stainless-steel vanity that heralds the passage into the washing areas.

Despite the cool and bare qualities of the materials used, the constant presence of aluminum and concrete lend a certain depth and warmth to the space. The effect of light on these surfaces renders reflections that are as subtle as they are theatrical, searching for that balance between discipline and drama which characterizes this sleek and stylish bachelor pad.

Both halogen and flourescent fixtures are used in a variety of combinations to define the function and mood of each space.

The light underneath the shallow slate steps creates a luminous glow, luring one into the sumptuous bath area.

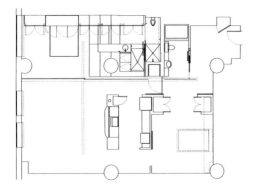

General floor plan

Left: The module along the bedroom wall incorporates extractable cupboards with built-in lights and fold-out compartments that remain concealed and discreet when closed.

Below: The translucent sliding glass doors feature a clear horizontal strip that offers the fortunate voyeur a strategic view of the bathtub.

metal

GREENHOUSE EFFECT
Sidnam Petrone Gartner

Architect: Sidnam Petrone Gartner, hansberry@aol.com   Photographer: © Michael Moran   Location: Harrison, New York, USA

This weekend residence is a much welcomed escape from the nearby chaos of New York City, nestled in a patch of richly dense woods over a bed of undulating terrain. The structure crops up as if from out of the rocks, seemingly rooted in a tamed landscape. Stone walls and an intricate steel framework sustain this spacious and luminous interior.

The 1.5 acre site sustains a multi-level structure with slanting roofs that mimic the top-ographical character of the land. Hugged by a cluster of trees at its back, a great two-story living room looks out through full height steel-framed windows towards the most prominent rock feature and a clearing. This breathtaking room evokes the feeling of a greenhouse, be-ing engulfed as it is by the foliage and sheltered underneath such a tall ceiling. The steel structure is left exposed and allowed to penetrate beyond the envelope in order to height-en the distinction between natural and man-made. A sloped butterfly roof sheltering the en-trance, master bedroom, living room and kitchen emphasizes the transition between levels. A second volume that locks into the north end of the main building contains a garage, mud room and master bath on the lower floor and guest bedrooms on the top floor. A terrace sus-tained by pillars extends from this vertical structure, this end of the project counterbalanced by a chimney on the south side.

In the endeavor to embrace the qualities of the landscape, stone translates into the structure as well as the interior of the residence. Sandstone walls and stone tile floors lie between the steel framework, linking the surrounding rocks that border the home with the elegant living spaces.

Above: A metal staircase leads to two bedrooms and a guest suite. The bedroom opens onto the large terrace seen from the exterior.

Opposite: The perforations of the steps and the fine cables that sustain the rails provide transparency, emphasizing this quality which is so significant to the great room.

The metal structure can
also be seen from outside.
Above: A view of the main
entrance.

metal

IN SUSPENSE
Peanutz Architekten

Architect: Peanutz Architekten, grille@berlin.snafu.de   Photographer: © Thomas Bruns   Location: Kreuzberg, Berlin, Germany

This Berlin loft was built to take advantage of a gap that was left by an old staircase inside a telephone factory. Its high ceilings and vertical potential prompted the architects to take advantage of the space and convert it into a multi-level loft. A mix of materials including wood, glass, brick and metal come together to form a dynamic space, most notably a metallic mezzanine.

A surface area of 1,320 square feet was distributed on three levels. The entrance, near the kitchen, which forms part of the building's original stairwell, opens onto a twenty-three-foot-high space. The open-plan kitchen is contained within a U-shaped module of cabinets and drawers, and beyond is a dining table with views through glass doors to the exterior. A kitchen closet was designed to incorporate steps that lead up to the second level—a steel mezzanine structure containing the bedroom that suspends from a series of steel beams. On the other side, a main staircase, also in steel, leads to the gallery on the third floor. A bridge joins this space to the bedrooms, the office and the library, while another staircase leads to the sitting room.

The solution provided by the hovering structure is one that isolates the sleeping area by using the vertical space and eliminates the need for allocating one whole level to a bedroom, which would ultimately inhibit the transparency between levels and the amount of light that reaches the interior. It allows for the spaces to remain open and uncongested, while maintaining a feeling of privacy within the bedroom due to its robust and thick composition. The structure suspends just above the kitchen, keeping the area visually isolated from the cooking area and free from any direct smells, fumes or noise. The use of steel is also an attractive finish that refers to the industrial character of the original surrounding space.

Another bedroom is contained within a similar space as the steel mezzanine, accessed by the main staircase that originates on the lower floor. A vaulted ceiling stands over the living room area.

A network of metal beams and railed lights are fixed along the brick walls, carefully illuminating the interior spaces.

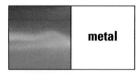

metal

THREE CYLINDER HOUSE
Makoto Tanaka

Architect: Makoto Tanaka   Photographer: © Makoto Tanaka   Location: Tokyo, Japan

An unconventional allocation of space often leads to imaginative and interesting forms and concepts. In this house located in the quiet residential area of Tokyo´s Setagaya district, architect Makoto Tanaka chose to erect three cylindrical pods in which certain functions of the home were to be allocated. He did so using metal as the defining element, creating imposing yet sleek figures that configure a dynamic interaction between the different areas of the house.

The designer seems to have been attracted by the simplicity of these elements, which can be interpreted as trees stripped down to their basic form. An open plan living area incorporates these three volumes, one containing the kitchen, the other a bathroom and the other a spiral stairway. Each of them can be opened up to communicate with the surrounding area, or closed off to conceal the units from sight. The wood floors on the lower level are broken by a walkway guided by a series of round spotlights integrated directly into the floor. The three cylinders are linked by a metal grated surface which connects to an area upstairs.

The project unites very Japanese qualities: the compartmentalization of functions into small spaces, the simplicity of gestures and the significant use of specific materials. In this case, the compartments are part of an open and luminous space, keeping the home from being cluttered in any way. They take the place of the conventional room, serving a function as well as an aesthetic and conceptual purpose. Despite their physical simplicity, they are still dramatic and symbolic in their form. Much of this is thanks to the material employed in furnishing them, creating smooth and reflective surfaces that are as discreet as they are theatrical.

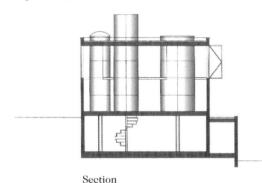

Section

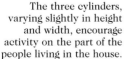
The three cylinders, varying slightly in height and width, encourage activity on the part of the people living in the house.

metal

TIN HAT
Artec Architekten

Architect: Artec Architekten   Photographer: © Margarita Spiluttini   Location: Raasdorf, Austria

A former farmhouse in need of a structural makeover, this home in the rural town of Raasdorf, Austria belongs to a farmer and philologist. The owner wished to have a space where he could dedicate time to both his professions, a space for agricultural tasks as well as a modern space for his own personal library. The challenge faced by the architects was to introduce a contemporary extension that would enclose the library and still preserve the rural character of the original structure.

The architects chose to conserve the brick base unit, originally a stable and later converted into a living space, which frames the main entrance. They then replaced the pieces in danger of collapsing with a smooth and reflective aluminum façade that delineates the access to and space dedicated to the library. This structural element was meant to separate the two functions of the house and still maintain a cohesiveness between the two spaces.

The prefabricated aluminum panelling connects the metal bay at the foundation and unites both constructions by way of a staircase on one side of the rear façade. The reflective aluminum structure makes its way up and culminates in an upper level that looks out through large glass doors onto a decked terrace, which is the roof of the main brick structure. The geometric extension is voluminous, yet its lightweight character lets it appear as if it were barely resting on the sturdy and worn brick base. Inside, the library is finished in light wood and, along with the bathroom, is very modern in keeping with its enveloping structure. The juxtaposition of prefabricated material and aged brick in a rural context creates a continuous dialogue between traditional and contemporary architecture that brings the two together in spite of all their differences.

The aim of the architects was a result that would satisfy the owners' needs, both functional and aesthetic, without seeming artificial or imposing on the surrounding landscape.

Opposite: Nearly all surrounding views are obscured from the library, which is flooded by light through apertures in the walls and ceiling that channel the natural light in and around the space.

The minimalist bathroom is naturally lit by a long narrow skylight that runs the length of one wall. This element was designed with the secondary purpose of collecting rainwater.

metal

THE SPACESHIP
Bart Prince

Architect: Bart Prince   Photographer: © R. Borden, L. Wilson, C. Mead   Location: New Mexico, USA

This residence is located along the banks of Jémez Springs in New Mexico. The project is the result of a close collaboration between the owners—a couple in search of a peaceful rural abode—and architect Bart Prince, who was able to fulfill the domestic needs of his clients and to materialize their general concept. The building finds itself sheltered in a semi-arid landscape, bordering the edge of the Jémez River and backed by rugged mountains and scores of poplars.

The structure lifts off the ground, supported by pine posts in case of flooding, and rests on a platform made up of a laminated wood beam framework. A central staircase rises up through the center of three floors of the symmetrical house. The lower level contains the common areas including the kitchen, office, living and dining room and a guestroom. The bedrooms occupy the second level, while the third level boasts a spectacular balcony.

The unique nature of the materials and the construction details employed in the project makes for a singular and unordinary residence. The outer walls are covered in corrugated metal siding, and the balcony railings are slender metal slats supported by uprights that unify them vertically. The galvanized metal and glass staircase rises above the façade, providing a vantage point from which to take in the splendid views. The characteristics of the metal structure form a recurring horizontal pattern that is reinforced by the clear establishment of each individual floor, while the texture of the metal finish reflects the sunlight in a multitude of ways, giving the house a certain futuristic appearance. It is not surprising then, that the neighboring residents have dubbed it "the spaceship", while passersby stop along the road to marvel at the unique and peculiar home.

Bart Prince´s design materialized out of a concept that adapts to the needs of its tenants and reflects the forms and shapes of the mountains and deserts of the New Mexico landscape.

Left: The slatted metal balconies and supporting wooden framework forge a complex and intricate pattern that adds a dynamic quality to the structure.

Opposite, center: The main façade differs from the rear in that the translucent glass-faced staircase protrudes from the metal frame, forming successive futuristic-like compartments through the center of the building.

Opposite, bottom: As well as reducing the risk of flooding, the elevation of the structure on wooden posts creates transparency, allowing the vast expanse of the land to be seen through the house.

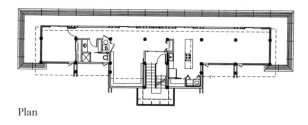

Plan

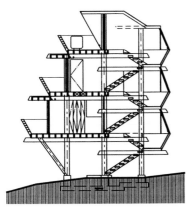

Transversal section

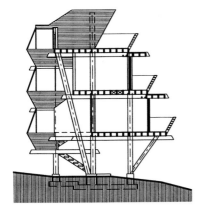

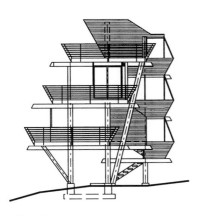

Elevations

metal

REFRACTION HOUSE
Kiyoshi Sey Takeyama

Architect: Kiyoshi Sey Takeyama, amorphe@nn.iij4u.or.jp   Photographer: © Yoshio Shiratori   Location: Nagoya, Japan

The construction of single-person houses has become very common in Japan. These spaces tend to be elongated, continuous and open-plan. This house was commissioned by the owner of a restaurant, a bachelor, and built in a typical residential area on the outskirts of Nagoya. Its outer shell is entirely composed of inclined metallic siding, its lateral sides in zinc and the façades in oxidated steel. A rectangular concrete tower at the back balances the main areas, linked to each other by a glass passage.

While the principal space contains the bachelor´s residence, the lower floor of the tower is dedicated to receiving guests. The guest bathroom is located on the upper floors. The walls of these areas are painted white, while the floors feature a variety of materials: ceramic tiles, wooden panels, tatami mats, polished concrete, and bamboo canes.

The metal-clad structure belies the existence of such a light-filled and basic interior, adorned with sparse furnishings and lined in raw materials. Windows are recessed into the walls, taking on unusual shapes along the inclined walls and ceilings. Sliding doors and the change in flooring distinguish the different areas of an otherwise uninterrupted space. Individual elements such as the kitchen and bathroom counters, the slanted columns and the long walkways emphasize the simplicity and strength on which this residence is built. These characteristics are further enhanced by its unique exterior composed of discreet forms, refined detail and ultimately its visual impact: its structure bending just as a light beam refracts under water.

These triangular skylights recall the angularities that recurr throughout the entire residence. A long passageway that runs along the wall is clad in glass to permit the movement of light.

View of the Refraction
House at night: The
window lights up, as if
an eye is peering out and
keeping watch.

Wood: organic fibers

Advantages: previously plentiful and cost-effective, easy to work with, moderately strong in compression and tension

Disadvantages: no longer plentiful or cost-effective, rots, swells and burns easily

It is often forgotten that wood dwellings date as far back as those in stone, having been used by the early Egyptians to build pyramids and by the Greeks to construct their temples. In fact, many stone buildings were simply imitations of earlier wooden structures. Centuries of fires and wars, however, have destroyed most wooden buildings, leaving little for archaeologists to discover and document. Wood is widely used in residential construction yet a highly controversial material for its ecological repercussions. Nevertheless, innovations in wood architecture are providing ways of renewing and prolonging its lifespan so that it is not wasted or thrown away. The material's versatility allows architects to mold it into any shape and to use it in practically any climate. Being a great insulator of heat, it is often used in colder climates for its thermal conductivity. Parquet is one of one the most common and sought after flooring for its look and comfort. A multitude of types of wood are available to create a specific mood, texture or color. If we learn to use it wisely and in appropriate quantities, it will continue to be the product of beautiful contemporary homes.

wood

wood

THE RED HOUSE
Jarmund / Vigsnæs

Architect: Jarmund / Vigsnæs, jva@jva.no Photographer: © Nils Petter Dale Location: Oslo, Norway

Amidst a picturesque landscape and a not-so-welcoming climate lies this Norweigan home which seems to have sprung out of a modern fairy tale. Rarely are we witness to a home that stands out of its surroundings, most especially through its color rather than it form. Far more used to the neutral shades granted by natural wood, steel, brick, and concrete, etc., this house is a welcome change to the monotony. This all-wood home appears like a mirage in the desert, only the other way around: a warm, inviting refuge from the stark and snowy winter.

The site on which the house is constructed is a former garden on the east bank of a river. The building is placed perpendicular to the stream to heighten the drama and to avoid obstructing the views of the house beyond. The rectangular structure rises over a glass corner and folds over itself to create a covered terrace. Red was the color chosen for the exterior walls, in deference to the wishes of the client. Inside, the finishes are light and smooth. White walls, light wood and translucent glass predominate. The living room and kitchen share the same space, separated only by the counters that delineate the kitchen area. A fireplace occupies the far corner. The ambience is warm and comfortable enough to make you forget that the snow outside is cold and wet.

The living spaces are situated on the top floor, orientated towards the spectacular views, while the lower floor houses the bedrooms, which face the river valley to the north. This double orientation dictates the architectural gesture conveyed by the structure. Like the shape of the number five, the two floors are configured so that they enjoy alternative views of the landscape. The terrace upstairs provides a panoramic view through a horizontal slit, protected overhead from the fall of snow. The project is like a magical home, its color a beacon that welcomes the home owner to a warm and protected haven.

A different way of seeing: Wooden ceiling beams stop short of the windows and descend onto a ledge, offering framed views of the exterior.

View of the staircase that leads down to the bedrooms.

This perspective allows us to
see the way the structure folds
over itself, creating a double-
perspective of the landscape.

wood

PRODIGY
Satoshi Okada

Architect: Satoshi Okada, okadas@cb.mbn.or.jp   Photographer: © Hiroyiki Hirai   Location: Norusawa Village, Japan

Satoshi Okada´s enigmatic project rises from the ground amidst the densely green hills of Mount Fuji like a looming shadow. The building sits on what was in the past a rugged volcanic terrain that settled and over time became smooth grassy hills sprouting with deciduous plants and tall trees. The long plot extends northeast-southwest, and sustains a geometric composition of angular walls and sloping ceilings.

The all-encompassing presence of wood in the landscape drove the architect to build with this material to create a harmony between architecture and nature. The monumental structure, furnished out of black-stained cedar, hides in the midst of the forest like a dark secret. Its sombre appearance is deceiving: a white and lumimnous residence awaits inside, full of windows, skylights, terraces and spacious rooms. A diagonal wall that runs through the building divides the house into two sections: a large open space designated for the living area and domestic functions, and the other for the bedrooms and bathrooms. At the entrance, a long corridor slowly opens out to a great gallery that contains the living room. Adjacent, under a lowered ceiling, a small loft accomodates the kitchen and dining room. A small hall leads to the bedrooms on the other side.

The use of wood in this project is an architectural solution as well as a symbolic reference to its surrounding landscape. While inside, the wood floors are a light oak parquet to enhance luminosity, the exterior has been tinted a dark tone to blend in with its environment. The structure has the appearance of being firmly rooted to the ground, as are the countless trees that envelop it. A poetic exercise for the architect, the project speaks for itself in a contemporary, timeless and mystical tone—an architectural feat camouflaged amid the foliage.

The kitchen/dining area is barely six and a half feet in height, whereas the living room extends to sixteen and a half feet. The difference creates a perceptual division of the two areas.

Below: Strategically placed skylights cast bright reflections of light across the interior walls and floors.

Below right: The bathroom floors were finished in granite instead of wood for practical reasons.

The angular shape of the
house gives it an ominous and
mysterious appearance.

COZY CABIN
Wingårdh Arkitektkontor

Architect: Wingårdh Arkitektkontor, wingardhs@wingardhs.se   Photographer: © Åke E:Son Lindman   Location: Skåne, Sweden

This small villa, previously a mill that formed part of a farm, is located in a small town outside of Malmö, in Sweden. The house is one of a series of buildings that inhabit both banks of a small stream. Engulfed by a charming setting of abundant trees and fallen leaves, the property is protected by a stone wall that lends privacy to the glass-fronted interior. The intimacy of the refuge is further enhanced by its fully wooden finish.

The house is divided into two levels, and takes advantage of the high pitched roof to insert a bedroom into a mezzanine. The common area downstairs includes the living room, kitchen, bathroom and sauna. The integration of a sauna led to the creation of additional spaces, including a room in which to relax before entering the sauna and a small exterior pool designated for the therapeutic ritual of taking a cold dip after each session. A concealed stairway leads to the bedroom, whose unique characteristics afford two triangular walls beneath steeply sloping ceilings. Everything except for the glass and concrete fireplace and the stone floor downstairs is lined in a light natural wood. In certain areas, such as on the furniture and behind the bed, the wood has been given a different grain with the use of smaller planks to contrast these spaces from the main supporting walls.

From the exterior, the house has the appeal of an invitingly warm cabin. Its doors open out onto a platform that stands over the water of the passing stream. A roof covered by small shingles of slate evokes its agricultural past and the glass walls and comfortable modern interior add a contemporary touch to a rural home—a small and enchanting sanctuary in the middle of Sweden´s picturesque countryside.

Top: The ceiling intended to separate the loft from the living area is supported by a network of beams. The kitchen area is defined by a raised floor level, accessed by two steps.

Far left: The kitchen is enclosed only by its furniture units, remaining open to the living area.

Left: A deep, round opening acts as an original window, letting in light and allowing a pinhole view of the outside.

Opposite: The overwhelming presence of wood in the bedroom requires little else in the way of decoration: a comfortable bed, a shelf, and intimate lighting are just enough for a room that looks out through a great triangular window at a beautiful setting of trees.

205

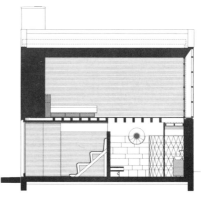

Sauna section

wood

TRANSPARENT CANVAS
Pachi Firpo

Architect: Pachi Firpo Photographer: © Ricardo Labougle Location: Uruguay

This spectacular house on the coast of Uruguay takes the potential of its stunning landscape and turns into the main feature around which the home revolves. A perfectly modern and minimalist space that finds inspiration in the colors that surround it; sand, sea and sky give way to light, dark, and white woods that come together to make the views the main attraction.

The rectangular plan of the house focuses its energy in the center, where a series of horizontal and vertical beams act as a canopy over the living area and exterior patio. The kitchen/dining room and bedroom/bathroom are found on either side of the lounge area, which is enclosed in glass to maintain a continual presence of the abounding blue water. The wooden deck behind features a cross-shaped pool that completes the chromatic syncronization with the landscape with its bright blue hue. Split-cane slats make up the canopy-like roofs over the deck, offering shade and diffusing light. A frontal view of the house demonstrates the importance placed by the architects on the beautiful views of the sea; the glass walls between which the lounge is located, trimmed in a pale cream, perfectly frame the Atlantic shore and puts each individual element into perspective.

While the exterior walls and living structures are concrete, the overall material used is wood, implemented both functionally and aesthetically. Aside from making up the framework and defining the different zones, the interplay of beams creates a dynamic dialogue between architecture and landscape. The exterior framework and deck are finished in a darker wood, while inside the wood floors and furnishings become white-washed and take on a more solid texture. A combination of rustic details and minimalist color within a contemporary structure are what characterize this light-filled refuge along the South American coast.

Below: Light wood dominates in the interiors: the floors, windows and kitchen furniture reflect light off of their light, white-washed surfaces.

Below right: The bathroom was placed independently on one side of the house and furnished with just the necessities in order to save space. A window always makes sure that the ocean remains in view.

wood

A RUSTIC PALACE

Photographer: © Alan Weintaub   Location: Carmel, California, USA

Aesthetically perhaps more evocative of the countryside than the beach, this house in California grounds itself on the use of wood to create comfortable and practical interiors. The austerity of the cubic structure is softened by the weather-beaten quality of the wood it is made of, whose form and texture lends a vertical dynamic to the house. The building is structurally self-contained and surrounded by a wood plank fence that offers privacy and still allows perfect panoramic views of the sea.

The various rooms within the house are formed by a succession of cubes that are all in contact with the exterior. Unvarnished pine and other kinds of wood are the backdrop for an original combination of styles and other building materials. Inside, planks of pine line the ceiling, walls and some of the floors and also take the form of beams and columns that delineate the different areas. Stone tile floors, metal grating and concrete bricks are some of the other materials present inside the house, which complement a mix of simple furniture with other more detailed and exquisite pieces that give character to the home.

While the lower level contains the living areas, the upper level contains the bedrooms, separated by a large glass shower. In each area an elegent canopy bed shrouded by translucent white fabric is placed against the windows. Outside, the decked terrace is protected by the enclosure, although various openings in the wooden structure peer out onto the landscape as if there were a canvas. The project is a splendid example of how typically rustic woods can be combined with other materials and styles to achieve an eclectic and unique environment.

The tall ceilings are perforated with skylights to let in natural daylight. The windows take on a vertical and linear motion as do many of the elements that make up the interior and exterior structure.

A narrow space is turned into a bedroom by placing a bed alongside the window and creating privacy by way of a canopy.

Different tones of wood mingle with metal floors and glass walls side by side.

wood

ROUND AND ROUND
Mario Connio

Architect: Mario Connio, m.connio@stl.logiccontrol.es   Photographer: © Ricardo Labougle   Location: Punta del Este, Uruguay

This unique complex in Punta del Este, Uruguay is a refuge surrounded by water and composed of natural materials that originate from the area. The complex is made up of three separate cabins placed on an octagonal wooden deck whose center is strategically placed to gather the moonlight. The three subtly curved structures are glass-fronted to collect natural light and are built out of tropical wood, reed and cane.

The largest cabin contains the living room, kitchen and service area. Another houses a studio, master bedroom and bath, while the third, with two small bedrooms and baths, is reserved for guests. The wood that covers the deck continues throughout each cabin, uniting all three spaces and forming a small central patio which is the heart of the complex. Three trees, each planted in front of one of the cabins, reinforces the presence of wood and nature. On one side, close to the edge, a curved pool follows the circular motion of the deck.

Inside, it is difficult to find any object or structure that isn't made out of wood. The pitched ceilings are held up by reed and beams of cane, while the walls are the same as the boarded floors. The blinds are also made out of reed and are held up by a thick string. A large old-fashioned iron fireplace inside the master bedroom is practically the only structure of another material. Slightly different shades of wood come together with neutral colors to create a very tranquil and overall natural environment that was inspired by nature and the materials it has to offer.

The circular deck is used as an open-air dining area, where the roof is made of split cane that provides protection from the sun and still lets light through.

The octagonal shape of the cabins imply a slow, meticulous building process that had to take into account the characteristics, possibilities and limitations of using wood as the single source for construction.

A walkway marked by cane structures guides a small path towards the shore.

wood

PIECES OF A PUZZLE
Jarmund / Vigsnæs

Architect: Jarmund / Vigsnæs, jva@jva.no   Photographer: © Nils Petter Dale   Location: Nesodden, Norway

Perched on top of a rocky hill that looks out over the land and sea, this project consists of a concrete base topped by a structure wrapped in wood. Located on a peninsula in the Oslo Fjord, this city in Akershus County is an artists' colony. The region boasts beautiful beaches, art galleries, and magnificent scenery. Apart from taking advantage of these features, the area is so calm and easy-going that there is not much else to do other than enjoy life.

A trail of concrete steps through rock, dirt and trees leads up to the main entrance of the home. The building is composed of two main entities: a rectangular body that houses private areas and a second volume that locks into one of its corners which contains the common areas and an open terrace. The walls of the structure act as a coating over the windows which interrupt the continuous wood surface. Light and narrow wooden planks are set in a vertical direction, emphasizing the precipice on which the house stands.

Inside, the living area is delineated by a wood floor and the kitchen and dining area by white tiles. An enclosed space within the living room contains the bathroom and storage. Shelves were incorporated onto a shelf underneath the ceiling, creating a space areas free of clutter. Cooking is hardly a chore when served with stunning views such as those seen from the kitchen and dining area. Full-height glass doors open onto a spacious wooden deck terrace with a small table and chairs. From outside, the house comes together like two pieces of a puzzle, interlocking to form one cohesive element unified by its wood composition. It fits just as easily into its native landscape, adapting to its movement and embracing its beauty.

On the edge: The house's high position allows for the privileged views obtained from every vantage point.

Rows of horizontal windows contrast with the vertical planks that make up the structural walls.

Light: natural and artificial

Although not a material per se, light is a crucial component of any contemporary home. Without it, the materials and objects that compose the spaces will be muddled and may go unnoticed. Without it the home will feel enclosed, isolated and grim. Houses with large windows and plenty of light breathe energy, highlighting the interior spaces and even making them appear larger. There are numerous ways of bringing light into the home. Depending on the way natural light is manipulated, a space can take on a whole new meaning. The shapes of windows, where they are situated and how they are distributed contributes to the desired mood. Skylights, terraces, glass doors and translucent materials are only some of the ways in which light can be conducted. Artificial light is also a very important decorative resource. In the same way as daylight, it can be controlled through a variety of forms and materials to afford the luminous, comfortable and relaxing home that everyone desires.

light

light

WALLS OF LIGHT
Noboyuki Furuya / Studio Nasca

Architect: Noboyuki Furuya / Studio Nasca, mo-a@po1.dti2.ne.jp   Photographer: © Mitsuo Matsuoka   Location: Tokyo, Japan

This is the private home of the architect who designed the house, located in a residential part of Tokyo's Setagaya district. The L-shaped building embraces a beautifully landscaped garden sprouting with trees and plants and laid with stone paths. The objective of the project was to allow as much light as possible into the interior spaces.

To do so, virtually every exterior wall was faced in glass from top to bottom. The simplicity of the structure—two rectangular blocks joined at right angles—made this procedure an easier task. Long panels of glass trimmed at equal lengths by vertical wooden posts compose one of the façades, while the other glass wall is punctuated by wider wooden panels. The narrow wooden supports unite with wooden beams that run across the white ceiling of the interior. Before reaching the inside of the home, sunlight passes through tree branches and leaves, casting innumerable moving shadows upon the wood floors. The effect is of a large sunroom where one can relax and take in the daylight hours.

As well as making it visually pleasing, the architect made sure that practicality formed part of the project's design. The main bedroom, along with the children's room, is separated from the remaining space by partitions, which, like the furniture, are easily removable should the need arise to create a single, large area. The building structure and its foundations, which incorporate thick planks, are also earthquake resistant and insulated from noise and fire. The project brings together the beauty of nature, the continuity of space and the functionality of architecture into a beautiful, light-filled residence.

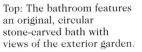

Top: The bathroom features an original, circular stone-carved bath with views of the exterior garden.

Opposite: The bathroom, with its high, sloped ceilings, conveys the sensation of being suffused by an expanse of warm, diffused light.

A noctural view of the house demonstrates that not only is it designed to receive light, but also to give it off light as if it were a lantern amidst the trees.

light

VERTIGO
Gerold Wiederin

Architect: Gerold Wiederin   Photographer: © A. T. Neubau Location: Dornbirn, Austria

This house is located in the beautiful town of Dornbirn in the Austrian region of Vorarlberg, known as the setting for many important architecture projects. Northwest of the home is a vast meadow and south is a house that belongs to the owner's parents. As a way of taking advantage of the location's views and natural light, the architect placed the building at the edge of an incline.

The three-story structure conceals one of its floors underground. The remaining two are staggered so that a balcony becomes part of the rear. The main façade looks west, creating views of stunning sunsets from the inside. Both eastern and western façades are finished in glass, while the northern and southern sides are closed except for two medium-size windows. Coated with a greenish-gray mineral mixture, the brick wall and its pigments produce reflections that create an iridescence when in contact with the sun's rays. The presence of light is also significant within the house. Large glass doors display panoramic views from the lower level, where a wooden core that contains the installations and means of access forms part of a continuous, open space strategically divided by sliding doors. A polished concrete floor unifies the entire level. The upper level features a corridor that leads to the private areas.

The use of light wood and polished concrete creates a warm and inviting interior that contrasts with the cold and heavy exterior. The thoughtful orientation of the structure and the extensive glass panels allow for an even and profuse distribution of light throughout the home, enhanced by reflective surfaces and warm materials such as light, natural wood.

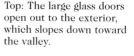

Top: The large glass doors open out to the exterior, which slopes down toward the valley.

Above: The upstairs corridor that runs north to south is to be converted into a library.

Left: One of the windows on the side of the home belongs to the bathroom, where a large bathtub lined in wood boasts views of the white landscape.

Opposite: The floor plans demonstrate the unique irregular shape of the project's roof.

Western elevation   Cross-section   Northern elevation

light

MENU OF THE DAY
Cristina Rodríguez + Augusto LeMonnier

Interior Designers: Cristina Rodríguez + Augusto LeMonnier Stylist: Ino Coll Photographer: © Pere Peris Location: Girona, Spain

This former restaurant in Girona, Spain was fully restored into a spacious and comfortable two bedroom house. The structure is composed of two levels, its entire façade punctured with windows to flood the interior with as much daylight as possible. Almost every surface is white or light grey so that the main feature of the space is its luminosity.

A variety of materials make up the space: varnished wood, painted walls, stone tiles, dark wood and natural rugs are the backdrop for measured doses of intense color in the form of fabrics, cushions, and flowers. The ample ground floor is spread out into a living and dining area and kitchen that receives all the exterior light that comes in through the façade windows. The dominant feature is doubtless the minimalist fireplace whose large structure demands a great deal of visual attention. The coolness of the stone and predominance of white is set off by the twin-size velvet floor cushions that lie facing the fireplace, as well as the sturdy rectangular table and teak benches that sit in the dining area. Upstairs, the master bedroom is just as luminous, with added color, texture and practical features that are necessary within a bedroom space.

The solid sukupira wood staircase is unobtrusive in the surrounding space, and provides a contrast that balances the lightness and neutrality of the house. Windows along the staircase keep this passage illuminated and the white walls bounce the light through to the upstairs. Peculiar furniture, a mixture of antique and modern yet never overpowering, add stylistic touches to the interior. Oversized, translucent curtains preserve and enhance the quanitity and quality of light that imbues the home.

Top: Even the entrance door has been left in glass to optimize the amount of light that the home receives. This area was previously the dining terrace of the restaurant.

Left: The austerity of the fireplace is softened by the texture of velvet and the rounded shapes of the sofas, cushions and stools.

Opposite, above: A beautiful upright piano is one of the exquisite pieces in the house that subtly adds character and warmth to an otherwise neutral and linear theme.

Opposite, below: A lightweight fabric separates the bed from the dressing area—a practical alternative to a closet or closed-in storage space.

te: In reduzierter Schriftform auf abgehä
r Fassade illustriert sich der Slogan
: reduce to the max lautet die klare Botsc
. Eine große Videoinstallation und Soundcc
en empfangen den Besucher am Eingang mit
n rhythmischen Motiven und Sequenzen. Sie g
ben ihm Botschaften mit auf den Weg in

A practical solution: A lightweight
fabric separates the bed from the
bathroom area.

light

CURVES AHEAD
Antonio Fiol

Architect: Antonio Fiol   Photographer: © Stella Rotger   Location: Mallorca, Spain

Un espace dressé au coeur, c'est-à-dire de l'idée dans l'élément abstrait de la pensée, chaque matin repris en rêve,

Drenched in white light, this small 753 square-foot apartment exudes fluidity through its architectural forms. A play of volumes and organic lines runs throughout the apartment, unifying the different elements into one continuous theme. Curved lines and irregular shapes give a human feeling to the space, further emphasized by the amount of light that is channeled into every room.

The lack of many furniture pieces is due to the incorporation of the principal elements into the architecture. The irregular kitchen table held up by a metal structure, is made of polished concrete and an area behind it leads to the bathroom, located in what was previously an interior patio. A partition divides the bedroom from the kitchen area, the two visually linked by a transparent splashback on the kitchen counter. Accessible via the bedroom or entrance area, the bathroom is a platform covered in white tile into which the tub is recessed. The toilet was placed on the entrance side and the dressing room on the bedroom side for practical reasons. In the living room a continuous curvy cement platform attached to the wall serves as a base for the sofa, composed of big pillows. The theme of curved lines is echoed in the living room by two concave pillar-like structures that filter natural light between them as well as by the bookshelf design by Ron Arad.

The main priority in this apartment was given to the distribution of light. The bright white walls, natural cherrywood parquet and sparse furnishings contribute to the abundance of light and unity of space. The presence of flowers and vegetation gives purpose to this element and feeds energy into the luminous space. The recurring theme of undulating forms and precise materials aims to channel light in and around the entire apartment, flooding it with freshness and positive energy.

Plants form part of the interior design and are incorporated into the architecture itself. Flowerpots are placed on either ends of the cement sofa, framing and sheltering the sitting area.

Opposite: The bathroom has been raised to create a separate environment and to incorporate the unique bathtub. It is accessible via steps in the kitchen and bedroom.

In the kitchen, a small hole fixed into the counter acts as a bud vase.

Looking closely, one realizes that the kitchen splashback is in fact a window which frames a mural on the far wall of the bedroom that lies behind it.

En Architecture, j'aime la simplicité ; de même, en cuisine.

light

CLOSE BUT FAR
Legorreta Architects

Architect: Legorreta Architects, gagrisi@lmasl.com.mx   Photographer: © Lourdes Legorreta   Location: Monte Atros, Lamas, Mexico

Privacy was the main concern in this project, due to its location in a transitted commercial area west of Mexico city. In spite of this requirement, however, architects ensured a continuous communication between interior and exterior so that light and space would characterize this beaming refuge away from the bustle of the city.

The building was placed five meters from the street and three meters from the remaining property boundaries to comply with strict urban regulations and also to create a transition area from public to private. The structure is made private through a series of walls that conceal an exterior garden and terrace that directly link to the interior spaces. Divided along three levels, the bedrooms are located on the third floor, the living and communal areas on the second, and service areas in the basement. The patio affords light into the basement, while every other area has access to a porch, terrace or garden distributed around the rear of the house. The living areas on the ground floor are dispersed along different levels separated by steps, granting a distinctive passage between areas without the need for doors or partitions.

Skylights and windows in a multitude of sizes, heights and compositions infuse the house with natural light. White walls, stone floors and comfortable furniture are the backdrop for distinct contrasting tones and curious decorative objects. Tall trees and plenty of plants also maintain privacy and muffle the noise from the street. The clever positioning of windows, the concealed rear garden and pool and the access of each room to this exterior make this home a perfect retreat from the hectic urban context from which it emerges.

Top and right: A long hallway is punctured by openings that infiltrate sunlight. Bordered windows produce symmetric reflections that move across the interior surfaces as the day lingers.

Above: A tempting pool is visible from the bedrooms upstairs. It is made private by an exterior wall with climbing ivy that gives an oasis-like character to the patio.

Ground floor

Elevations

First floor

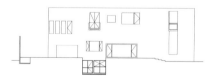

light

LIGHT BOX
Stephen Varady Architecture

Architect: Stephen Varady Architecture, svarady@bigpond.com   Photographer: © Stephen Varady, Russell Pell   Location: New South Wales, Australia

This residence is set on a grassy lot filled with trees and shrubs that become part of the architecture. Found in the beatiful location of Tea Gardens in New South Wales of Australia, the project was placed atop a hill to take advantage of the light and views. While the house receives an abundance of natural light, the artificial illumination inside plays a major role in the design and ambience of the home.

The two-story house is linked by a staircase that separates a garage, workshop and watertank downstairs from the living and bedroom zones upstairs. A bridge over a decline in the land links the garden to the upper level and leads to the living area and other rooms. An existing tree was incorporated into the bridge with the aim of integrating the surroundings into the architecture. The exterior was painted blue and grey, while inside some of the floors are polished concrete painted in black. The presence of blue and grey is repeated inside the home, along the walls and also in the form of light. In the kitchen, the storage units and counters are made of an acrylic material that when lit from inside creates a luminous glow-in-the-dark effect. The bathrooms also feature this design, complemented by an indirect fluorescent blue light that shines against the walls from behind long, horizontal mirrors. The effect is best appreciated at night, when the light takes on a more powerful and radiant appearance.

The construction of this residence involved an ecologically aware process that becomes evident in the technical and aesthetic solutions formulated to respect its surroundings and at once merge the two together. Light is manipulated in its natural form to bring as much of it as possible into the home, as well as artificially to create a unique interior that keeps on shining when night falls.

Right: The interior is decorated with simple furnishings, making daylight the primary feature by way of a glass-fronted façade that opens onto a broad terrace and floods the living areas with natural light.

Transversal section

light

GLASS INTERFACE
Edward Suzuki

Architect: Edward Suzuki, esa@edward.net   Photographer: © Katsuaki Furudate   Location: Tokyo, Japan

This complex comprises the client's family guesthouse on the lower two floors and their three respective residences on the upper floors. The theme of the design was to allow spacious terraces for each of the family residences, providing adequate privacy from the neighbors tightly surrounding the three adjacent sides. The façade is a combination of a glass screen and a cushion of green that acts as an interface between the building and the street, infiltrating diffused light into the spacious interiors.

The rooms inside consist of white walls and wood floors, always maintaining a relationship with the exterior via terraces, large windows or skylights. Tall trees planted into circular and rectangular white pots can be found throughout these areas, most notably in the covered terrace that looks out onto the street. The wood mesh from one of its lateral walls can be seen on the glass façade, occupying the place of one glass panel. The pleasant terrace features a high ceiling and small breakfast table with chairs. The floor consists of short and narrow wooden planks. Sliding doors and partitions serve to orientate the various areas of the residence. A large common room incorporates a glass ceiling supported by beams that continue along its glass doors. In the main living room, the floor area is distinguished by a light wood floor that is cut off at successive right angles by a white tiled floor, out of which emerges a spiralling staircase that leads to the bedrooms.

From the exterior, the glass panelling radiates a luminous glow, which translates directly into the interior spaces being filled with natural light. The use of clear glass within the rooms transports this light from one area to another, evenly distributing it throughout the residence. Light materials in light colors emphasize the lightweight character of the entire structure. At night, the whole building glows like a lantern amidst the neighborhood.

The glass walls are equipped with screens to protect the house from the direct sunlight and consequent heat.

Top: The living room features a recessed ceiling panel that emits a glowing indirect light from its borders.

Recycled: various materials

The advantages of recycled homes are self-evident. The disadvantages–if any–are ir-relevant. Besides being an environmental and resourceful form of architecture, it is al-so a driving force towards innovation, imagination and new ways of thinking. This century beholds a generation of architects that more and more are becoming part of a green movement in their profession. The result is a growing number of interesting projects that reflect ecological concerns and propose unusual and cutting-edge designs that revolutionize the concept of the home. The enormous amount of materials collected in landfills and illegal dumping sites from demolished buildings and discarded materials offers an infinite number of recycling opportunities. Architects and designers have learned to recognize these opportunities and transform them into unique and contemporary homes. Hopefully, this trend will gradually become a norm in architecture, granting a step forward in the restoration of the planet as well as the advent of original, alluring and modern living spaces.

recycled

THE SHED
Luis + Alvaro Fernández de Córdova Landívar

Architect: Luis + Alvaro Fernández de Córdova Landívar Photographer: © Jorge von Bergen + Gustavo Holguín Location: Santa Cruz, Bolivia

The starting point for this project was the acquisition of an old metallic shed structure and concrete water tank that were salvaged by the architects at a demolition site. These primary elements were integrated into the existing terrain surrounded by beautifully mature trees, while respecting the landscape and implementing ecological solutions.

With the intention of responding to the Amazonian-like climate of the region—very hot with abundant precipitation–the architects decided to recycle the structure of the abandoned shed so that it would act as a great parasol and umbrella. The distribution revolves around a home and studio, thereby allowing the installation of independent spaces and adding an urban characteristic to a space unified underneath a continuos roof structure. The scheme is divided in two: the north-south axis incorporates the most interesting section of the roof, and for that reason its view was left unobstructed from within by way of a large skylight. The east-west axis is defined by the water tank and a central, open-air-but-dry patio. A pool and fountain reinforce the direction of the axis and form the central elements of the composition.

The interior features high ceilings and well-lit spaces. Two impressive solid Caoba wood pieces, acquired by the architects many years ago, were used to serve as tables for the dining room and studio. The water supply as well as the pool are run on solar energy. These solar panels were placed on the west wing of the shed structure, making up another ecological factor defining this unique project.

The metallic shed roof measures 98 x 82 feet and was fabricated in Belgium. Strict measures were taken to assemble it on-site so that no damage would be made to the immediate surroundings.

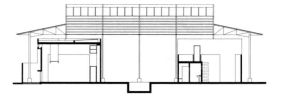

Cross-section

Cross-section

recycled

A LOT OF TANKS
Morton Loft LOT/EK

Architect: LOT/EK, info@lot-ek.com Photographer: © Paul Warchol Location: New York, USA

This unusual loft is located in what was previously the fourth floor of a parking unit in New York´s West Village. The project entailed the separation of private and public areas in a way that would refer to the location´s industrial origins. Its high ceilings and regular shape led to the idea of inserting two gas tanks inside the space and them into turning a bedroom and bathroom pod.

The tanks contain the most intimate rooms of the residence, leaving the rest of the space free for the living area and kitchen. One of the two modules was situated horizontally above the dining table and looks out over the living room and façade windows. The tank is comprised of two sleeping pods and is equipped with mattresses, spotlights and a hydraulic system that opens the tank with the flick of a switch. The second tank, placed vertically from floor to ceiling, houses two bathrooms—one on top of the other. A system of railings and metal grating catwalks leads to the loft, the bathroom on the second floor and the bedroom pods. This design enabled the architects to take full advantage of the space´s extensive height, leaving the ground floor clear of partitions. The interior design speaks the same industrial language as exterior renovation, using metal for furniture and a continuous enamel pavement on the floor. The presence of cement and exposed gas and electrical installations feeds the industrial character of the space. The lighting inside the tanks, the red furniture, and the blue floor add color contrast to the overall grey tones.

This is an excellent example of a project in which the term "loft" takes on a very meaningful definition. Remaining loyal to its past, the space is a materialized reference to its industrial origins, an imaginative and witty take on a living space. The prefabricated structures featured here are as original as they are aesthetic.

One can appreciate the sheer size of the tanks as they unite the four walls of the space both vertically and horizontally. The tanks confer a modern, high-tech aspect on the space.

The red furniture, orange lighting and blue floors offer an interesting chromatic relationship between the various areas.

The insertion of gas transport tanks into a living space was a clever adaptation of industrial equipment to domestic use. The bedroom pods were rid of ventilation grilles and fitted with a horizontal platform and hydraulic hatches.

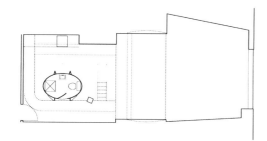

Ground floor

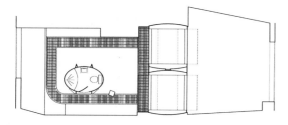

First floor

recycled

SLICK AND HAIRY
Sarah Wigglesworth and Jeremy Till

Architect: Sarah Wigglesworth and Jeremy Till, mail@swarch.co.uk   Photographer: © Paul Smoothy   Location: London, UK

Taking a closer look at this unusual residence and understanding the concept on which it is based will lead to a better understanding of its name. "Slick and hairy" is the term coined by the architects to describe this innovative construction, whose design favors time instead of fighting against it.

The home and studio lie in between the main East Coast railway line and a row of Victorian railway cottages on Stock Orchard Street in London. The L-shaped building contains in its long arm the office, and in the short section the living areas. The front gate is made of willow hurdles held inside a galvanized steel frame, juxtaposing a medieval and rural material with a contemporary and industrial one; refined and raw... slick and hairy. The office is supported on walls made of recycled concrete held in wire cages, which, despite their sufficient strength, were supplemented by columns cast in the center of each pier. A box of springs on top of each of these dampen the vibration from the passing trains. The sandbag wall features bags filled with sand, cement and lime tied back to a timber frame. Over the years, these bags will decay and the mixture will harden, forming a rippling wall of concrete left with the rough imprint of cloth—a challenge to the permanency of architecture. Two large water tanks, a composting toilet, solar panels and a condensing gas boiler further reflect the importance placed on recycling raw materials and saving energy.

Nine Stock Orchard Street can be seen from a distance, its curious exterior attracting attention from passersbys and its five-story tower acting as a beacon for its inhabitants. Not only is it a solidly ecological project that continuously evolves with the aid of time; it is also a modest and innovative venture that prides itself not on being novel or progressive, but on techniques that are simple, immediate and accessible.

Top: The straw bale window seen here was conceived as an exhibit in a science museum, revealing the secrets of the construction inside.

Straw is a cheap surplus material that provides a high insulation value.

Opposite: The bedroom wing is wrapped in straw bales behind shiny steel, uniting the slick with the coarse.

Nine Stock Orchard Street
is the first straw dwelling
to receive building control
approval and planning
permission in the UK.

THE FACTORY
Clinton Murray Architects Pty. Ltd.

Architect: Clinton Murray Architects Pty. Ltd., motu@acr.net.au   Photographer: © Janusz Molinski   Location: Marimbula. Australia

This house is constructed almost completely out of restored wood that was recycled from buildings constructed in the 1940's. Wood, one of Australia's most outstanding materials, is used to build infrastructures and large-scale constructions like bridges and piers. Because of wood's resistant character, the architect used it for the project's entire structural system. However, the floor supports and the window frames came from the demolition of old warehouses. The floors and complete pieces, such as doors, were recycled from an old wool factory.

The house's surroundings are typical of this part of the Australian east coast —a rough and hard environment. The home is organized according to a simple scheme in the form of a "U" that wraps around a patio that captures the morning sunlight. A 41-foot long swimming pool is protected from the neighbors on the lot's northern side by a fence constructed out of wooden strips. Generally used for the construction of oyster boxes, the strips pay tribute to the local culture, since oyster cultivation is the main industry of Merimbula. The fence also protects the patio from the south-west winds that prevail in the area. A large wooden terrace runs along the entire length of the building, on the side that looks towards the sea and receives the afternoon sun.

The climate in this part of Australia encourages residents to spend more time outdoors than indoors. As a result of this lifestyle and to strengthen the house's relationship with its surroundings, each room has ocean views and its own exterior space. Three guest bedrooms on the main floor are organized like a suite. The upper floor contains the master bedroom, a small living room, a dressing room, a bathroom and a large terrace.

The interior patio, the element that organizes and articulates all the spaces of the house, is an area of great sobriety and formal expressiveness. The openings towards this space are much more controlled than the large, continuous windows that open towards the exterior on the back façade.

Wood plays an important role in the interior. However, the floors are polished and varnished and the vertical partitions and the ceilings are plastered and painted white, creating a counterpoint to the materials on the exterior of the house.

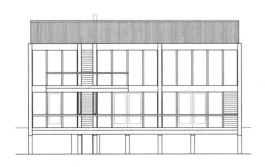

South elevation

The bedroom enjoys magnificent views of the ocean and incorporates its own private terrace beyond the floor-to-ceiling windows.

East elevation

recycled

RUSTY
Aaron Hojman

Architect: Aaron Hojman, aaronhojman@hotmail.com   Photographer: © Ricardo Labougle   Location: San Carlos, Uruguay

Amid a field of wild sunflowers sits this farmhouse inspired by the British train stations of the late nineteenth century and the traditional farms of North America. The constructive elements used, along with the solutions employed to decorate the interior, have been found in recycled materials obtained from abandoned sites and secondhand markets.

The house, barely 860 square feet, is located in the town of San Carlos in Uruguay, surrounded by a landscape of fields and far-off mountains. Intended as a temporary residence while its owner built his permanent home, the building became his regular country house, incorporating all the facilities and comforts of a contemporary home underneath an aged, vintage appearance.

The exterior structure was constructed with rusted metal panels rescued from abandoned train stations. The front entrance features a triangular glass door bought at an auction. A raised wooden platform in front of the entrance was made out of old planks that come from old bar floors. Rusty chairs that would otherwise be rubbish take on an attractive decorative character within this particular context. Likewise, the interior was decorated and furnished with articles found in markets, auctions and on road trips across the country. In fact, it is nearly impossible to find any piece, object or furniture that is not secondhand. On the living room table sits a globe that was given to the owner over thirty years ago by a Jewish family that had fled from Berlin. In the kitchen, antique sets of dishes come from old and stately hotels and mingle with ordinary tin containers and 1950´s appliances. A modest white bathroom contains a weather-beaten porcelain tub and two individual laundry-room style basins. A multitude of curious objects with a traceable past come together in this fully recycled and ultimately stylish country home.

Top: View of the triangular door fitted into the recycled metal structure, acquired from an auction of secondhand furniture.

Above: The varnished wooden chairs are a traditional model of a very typical chair found in many hotels in Uruguay.

The tables and closets in the kitchen also take on a vintage appearance through their cracked paint and worn finishes. Any imperfections have been retained to add character, creating a dialogue between the object´s past and its present context.

BACKYARD
Roto Architects

Architect: Roto Architects, roto@rotoark.com   Photographer: © Assassi Productions, Benny Chan, Tim Street-Porter   Location: Los Angeles, California, USA

What was once an electric company cabling structure north of downtown LA is now the home of a couple, one of whom is a builder and the other a dog breeder and trainer who is also active in the Los Angeles arts community. The clients were interested in accomodating their expanding collection of paintings and sculptures without compromising the privacy of their living space.

The stripped classical concrete and steel structure is surrounded by a yard that contains a collection of building materials and industrial artifacts collected from two generations of work and urban renovation. Many of these pieces were used in the construction of the new space. The singular yet complex construction is supported by a wave-like truss system which springs from a simple structural frame that bypasses the building shell to bear on six points—four on existing steel crane rails and two on the ground fifty feet below. Structurally, the new volume is completely independent from the existing industrial shell.

A series of volumetric elements, constructed with the recycled materials found on-site, includes a shield that protects the translucent kitchen and the interior from the sun, blocks the noise and dirt of the adjacent train switching yard and forms a protected vertical garden around an existing forty-foot-tall stand of bamboo. Cylindrical tanks, also from the backyard, were modified to make the pool, as well as a tower that acts as a light monitor, viewing platform and hot-air exhaust. This is topped by a small garden belvedere that is humidified by water mist. The ground floor is used as a semi-public garden and gallery space. The complex web of beams and interacting layers can also be appreciated from inside, which appears as a luminous, infinitely tall and dynamic space.

The sense of space is omnipresent: the height of the ceilings reminds one of the industrial origins of the structure. The living and sleeping areas are made more intimate by lowering the ceilings and providing panoramic views of the city.